pitfalls
and possibilities

A LEADERSHIP FABLE

KAREN MAIN

Pitfalls & Possibilities: A Leadership Fable
Published by Gertie-B Publishing
Copyright ©2021 by Karen Main. All rights reserved.

ISBN: 978-0-578-87599-6
BUSINESS & ECONOMICS / Leadership
Cover and Interior design by Wolf Design and Marketing, wolfdesignandmarketing.com

QUANTITY PURCHASES: Schools, companies, government entities, professional associations, clubs, and other organizations may qualify for special terms when ordering quantities of this title. For information, email k_main@msn.com.

To Audrey—and other unsung leaders

contents

author note

THIS STORY IS ABOUT Avery Daniels and Jon Ailey, two fictional characters who are compilations of the many interesting, smart, and often zany professionals I've encountered over the past years as a consultant and trainer. If you note a resemblance to yourself in any of the characters contained in this book, well, then you probably left a significant impact on me! But please rest assured that any resemblance to an actual person, organization, or situation is entirely unintentional.

This story is meant to educate on management and leadership principles; any inaccuracies regarding the technical components of accounting or utilities are solely mine and hopefully will not detract from the underlying intention of the book.

introduction

ARE CONGRATULATIONS IN ORDER? If you've made your way to this book, chances are you've recently been promoted to a leadership position. Perhaps this is your first time as a leader, and you're searching for an understanding of your new role. Or maybe you're an experienced leader looking for some fresh insights into how to lead a diverse team of people. No matter your level of experience, this book will give you a better foothold into how to lead, manage, and supervise others. Expect to learn current leadership practices and gain a solid foundation so you can be successful in your new position.

Some people—and I was one of them—believe that once you become a leader it means you've earned more: more status, power, skill, authority, more *whatever*. But that's really a misperception. Leadership isn't about finally proving to others how smart, capable, and important you are or about being held in high esteem. It's more than a title. It's a responsibility. Having the title of supervisor, manager, or CEO won't guarantee you credibility, status, or recognition. You've got to earn it by building trusting relationships with the individuals who report to you. That takes commitment and time.

Leading a team of people is an important role in our organizations today. Organizations accomplish things through people, and leaders balance the need to get things done while simultaneously supporting, encouraging, and empowering the people who show up to work each day. This balance calls for a shift in focus: from self to others. Leaders focus less on themselves and more on helping others accomplish their goals and succeed.

When you were an individual performer, your focus was on yourself and what you could achieve and accomplish. You studied your craft, invested in yourself through education, honed your skills, and demonstrated your competence through your abilities and expertise. We all try to make a positive name for ourselves by doing good work, and as individual performers, we seek promotions and advancements that make sense to us and our careers.

But as a leader, you're responsible for setting clear goals for the team and providing the resources, tools, guidance, and support they need to be successful. You might find yourself switching between accounting and scheduling to listening, congratulating, and thanking. Your team members will rely on you to stay focused; they will also count on you for feedback and coaching. You'll bounce from encouraging your team and cheerleading them on to helping them work through conflicts and disagreements. Leading a team is a remarkable opportunity to help others realize their own potential. It's often thankless and draining, but it can also be rewarding and satisfying!

Some people advance to a leadership position because they've proven themselves as technically strong. They know the organization and the ins and outs of their position, and they are viewed as a go-to person by other members of the team because of their knowledge or skill. In such cases, the natural progression is to promote this person to be the team's leader. Time after time, I've met employees who think technical expertise is all that's required of a leader. But leadership is much more than just telling people what to do. It's a highly relational role that requires exceptional communication and interpersonal skills, especially the ability to listen, empathize, and put others first.

Take a moment and give some thought to why you're here. Being promoted to a leadership position is often one of the only ways many of us earn more money in our jobs. Whether or not we really want to lead others, we take the job because it means more money and more prestige. If this is you, you're not alone.

However, if you're accepting a leadership position solely on the appeal of a better-paying salary, you may end up disappointed—and you may not be successful in your new role. You may, in fact, earn more money, but there are times when you'll work longer hours for your paycheck. As a supervisor or manager, you're taking on a heady combination of responsibilities and duties. No longer are you responsible only for your work. Instead, you're in charge of other people and can influence the trajectory of their careers, and hence, their livelihoods. If you're taking the position just for the money, you'll struggle with the need to empathize with your team members or give credit to others for the work they do. You may find it difficult to balance the need to be demanding with the need to be forgiving. If you're just in it for the money, you may find it hard to devote the time and energy necessary to build relationships with your team members.

Think twice, as well, if you've accepted the promotion because finally—finally!—you can start bossing people around the way others have bossed you. Being an effective leader isn't about using your newfound authority to command others. As enticing as it is to be in charge you'll find success difficult if you're just in it for power and prestige. The kind of power you're given as a leader is limited. Yes, you're given formal authority as a result of your promotion to supervisor or manager, but if you abuse this authority and use it for your own satisfaction or personal gain, you'll quickly lose credibility and respect from those around you. Your influence as a leader doesn't stem from power; it emerges as a result of the trusting relationships you've built with others. Respect and influence, in other words, come once you've established yourself as a trustworthy leader. Part of the purpose of this book, therefore, is to help you understand this distinction between "bossing" and "leading" others.

If you hope to be challenged by your new position, then hold on for the ride, because you'll be challenged in ways you never thought possible. You'll be asked to make quick decisions and solve problems. Sometimes you'll feel competent to solve problems, and other times you'll feel woefully out of your league. The most effective leaders realize they don't always have the right answers and will tap into the people around them for input, ideas, or help. You'll fill many roles when leading a team, including coach, teacher, and mentor. You'll help create opportunities for knowledge, ideas, and information to flow freely between and among people. You'll impact others by sharing your expertise as well as your willingness to learn from others. Continuous learning is at the heart of leadership.

As such, you'll learn more about yourself than you ever thought possible, gaining insight into your strengths, talents, and what makes you tick. You'll make plenty of mistakes but will, hopefully, learn from them too. The most effective leaders are honest, apologize when they mess up, and stay true to themselves. They don't try to be someone they're not, and they don't try to be everything to everyone. This type of vulnerability is not an easy thing for many of us who would prefer to avoid any hard reveals about our faults or failings. But when you step into leadership, you're a role model, "on display" for others who will watch to see how you manage your successes or cope with disappointment. I hope you'll be the kind of leader who "walks your talk" and lives your convictions.

If you want to effect change and positively impact others, I think you'll find the work of a leader rewarding, because you can be at the forefront of innovation, creative change, and new beginnings. You'll have the opportunity to consider new ways of doing things and decide on their efficacy. Sometimes it will make sense to challenge the status quo when it adds value, efficiency, or effectiveness to your organization, and sometimes it won't. Sometimes the initiatives you stand behind will be amazing! And sometimes they'll be huge flops.

Your role will very often be about helping others deal with change, be it incremental or dramatic. While most of us don't like change, as a leader, you have the responsibility to help others through it. As you help others cope with change and challenging times, you will help them discover new talents and abilities. Imagine: You will likely have a profound impact on the life of one, or many, of your team members. It doesn't get much more fulfilling than that.

The challenge of helping others fulfill their aspirations will open doors for you. If you focus on teaching, training, and developing your team members, you'll stand out for your efforts. The most successful leaders focus on building potential and capacity within their teams, and it's this focus that distinguishes the average leaders from the great ones. If you think back to a coach, teacher, or leader who made an impact on your life, it's most likely because they challenged you, gave you constructive feedback, and pushed you to do more than you thought you could.

By now, you might be realizing that leadership is more complex than you thought! Indeed, there is immense responsibility associated with leading a team. I've encountered far too many misinformed leaders—supervisors, for example, who didn't receive the right introduction to their role—who go on to hurt people's careers, damage relationships, and harm organizations. They didn't understand that leading a team is not about doing more and more of what you used to do, or bossing people around, or making employees do the grunt work, but is instead about doing a different kind of work: building relationships and serving others.

I decided to write this book to help new leaders, like you, understand—and in some cases, make—the transition from employee to leader. When I first stepped into a leadership position (many years ago), my ego got the best of me. I allowed myself to be disappointed by the performance of others, and I struggled with fairness, rewarding those who were driven like me and punishing those who weren't. Back in those days, I made a lot of mistakes and walked over a lot of good people. I'm sorry for those errors in judgment, but I'm grateful for the learning experiences because they made me more sympathetic to the leaders I work with today. Even now, I still have times when my ego leads instead of my brain (or my heart).

Over the course of many years, I've been privileged to lead both small and large teams. I've studied with experts and scholars in the field of leadership development. I've learned from great bosses and a few awful ones. I've studied book after book after book about what the gurus say makes for leadership excellence. I've coached and counseled hundreds of executives through tough situations. I've taught many new leaders, and some tenured ones, through my own custom leadership programs. I'm proud that these programs have successfully re-energized leaders and helped new ones bypass mistakes as they're just starting off.

This story is about Avery Daniels and Jon Ailey, two professionals beginning their journey as new leaders. The challenges they face, the decisions they make, and the lessons they learn are typical of the leaders I've met over the years. As you read through this book, think about how you might handle the situations Avery and Jon encounter. Ask yourself, would you respond differently and, if so, how? I encourage you to put yourself in Jon's and Avery's shoes and ponder your own reactions to the scenarios presented here.

To help you do so, each chapter includes reflection questions to challenge your thinking and explore your responses to the situations Jon and Avery experience. Before you start reading, grab a blank journal or notebook and use it to capture your thoughts and record any questions that arise for you as you read the story. You may also want to discuss the scenarios with your colleagues, boss, or family. This book will make a great companion to any leadership program or can serve as a jumping-off point for training classes.

Effective leadership is vital to the strength and sustainability of our workforce. With strong leadership, the possibilities are endless: We can improve organizational productivity, streamline processes, encourage innovation, strengthen relationships, and transform lives. As a leader, you'll likely encounter a few pitfalls along the course of your career, but if you approach your role with honesty, integrity, and humility, you'll sail through the rough spots and establish yourself as a credible leader.

Are you ready to experience the possibilities that leadership has to offer? Let's begin the journey.

chapter I

Starting off as a New Leader: Misguided Misperceptions

MOST OF US DON'T SEEK OUT a leadership position; we simply see a need and step up to fill it. That's what Jon Ailey did over the course of his career at Axion, a large industrial water utility in a bustling Midwest city. Jon began working at the utility as a young man. From his early beginnings as a part-time, seasonal employee he worked his way up the ladder to becoming a technician on field crews laying and fixing pipes, followed by a stint as a maintenance tech, with a promotion to utility crew leader, and finally, to his recent promotion to field supervisor. His current role puts him in charge of four crews responsible for maintaining water lines in the West-Side Corridor. His colleagues supervise similar crews in different areas of the city. His position is a fast-paced job that requires a high amount of technical expertise along with helpings of engineering, construction, and mechanical knowledge. His crews perform hard, sometimes tedious, and often dirty work, and not everyone is cut out for it. Those who do well are physically strong and bring a good amount of common sense and ingenuity, because not every solution to a problem in the field is clear-cut. It takes grit to work in the heat of the summer or the frigid temperatures of winter, hustling to repair outdated pipes or laying new ones. When asked what kept him in the job for so many years, Jon explained, "I like being able to solve different challenges each day, working with my friends."

For Jon, working at the utility was a family affair. Jon's father and grandfather worked at Axion, and this kind of patronage wasn't unusual. In fact, until recently, departments at Axion were made up of cousins and nephews and daughters and sons of employees. Members of the Ailey clan relied on Axion to provide for their families, and in return, they gave a good day's labor.

When the news broke that Jon's boss, Stuart Bradley, was being promoted, Jon knew he would apply for Stu's position. Jon wanted the promotion, partly for the bragging rights, but mostly for the bump in salary. Of course, there were others on the team who were just as qualified and eager for Stu's position. In municipal work, raises are usually reserved to cost-of-living adjustments, so being promoted into a leadership position is one of the few ways to earn more money. Jon knew he had stiff competition for the job but hoped his reputation as a hard worker, along with his technical skill, would earn him a spot on the candidates' list.

Jon possessed the necessary certifications for the job and was invited to the first round of interviews held with Stu, two representatives from HR, a manager from Engineering, and an Operations supervisor from a neighboring utility. The interview process was more complicated than he expected. Jon felt confident answering technical questions but stumbled on those related to employment matters, such as leave policies and employee relations. One question, "How would you deal with two crew members who didn't get along?" threw him. He thought his answer, "I would tell them to knock it off," probably didn't go over well with HR. Still, he wasn't surprised to make it to the final round of interviews, held with the director of Public Works, Patrick Lacey, and Stu.

"I did my best," he told his brother, a few days after the interviews were completed. He was hopeful but knew that his colleague, Emile Nelson, was a strong contender. Emile and Jon worked side by side over the last seven years. Emile held the same credentials as Jon but had a more easygoing temperament that made him much more popular with the rest of the crew.

When the phone call came from Stu, he took a deep breath. "It was a hard decision," Stu explained, sounding solemn, "but in the end we felt you are the best candidate for the position. Congratulations!"

Jon thanked him for his vote of confidence, and told him, "You won't be disappointed, Stu."

In typical Ailey fashion, his family threw a huge celebration in honor of Jon's promotion. Many coworkers attended, along with neighbors and Jon's extended family. His father bragged to everyone about his youngest son's accomplishment. "Just like his old man," Jon overheard him say to a neighbor. "He's going to go far at Axion."

Despite the show of encouragement, Jon couldn't help but worry. Stu, who led the department for more than a decade, was loved and respected by his crew members, who came to depend on his direct style. ("Have I ever left you guys hanging? Then why are you letting me down?") But the crew also knew his soft spots. ("Family is important, so take the rest of the week off after your grandma's funeral.") Jon knew he would be tested by the crew to see "how will he stack up against Stu?"

It would have to be a balancing act. His first concern was how he and Emile would get along now that Jon got the promotion that Emile also wanted. He and Emile went way back. Their kids went to school together. They were both on the same bowling league and often went fishing together. Emile, along with others from Axion, was a regular visitor to Jon's house for barbecues and Super Bowl parties. *A lot of these guys are my friends, and I don't want to mess that up*, Jon thought. He didn't want this promotion to change these relationships, but he also wanted to prove he had what it takes to run his crews. He wanted the respect that went along with the position.

As news of his promotion got around, Jon was grateful for the congratulations that came his way. He made it a point to seek out Emile. "Congrats, man," Emile offered.

"Yeah, thanks," Jon said, somewhat demurely. "Don't get me wrong," he continued, trying to soften any insult, "when Stu called and offered me the job, I said 'yes,' before he could figure out he was talking to me and not you." They bantered back and forth some more before Jon broached the subject of their future relationship. "As far as I'm concerned," Jon continued, "nothing needs to change between you and me."

Emile seemed to appreciate the gesture and agreed that they could continue to work together "like nothing changed."

"Maybe we can actually light a fire under some of these guys," Jon said. In the past, the two had many conversations over lunch complaining about the poor work ethic they saw from some crew members. Now that Jon was taking over at the helm, maybe he could fix some of those issues that drove him crazy for so long. For example, Stu never cared much about tardiness or sloppy work areas, but those things made Jon cringe. *Under my watch? People will come to work on time and clean up after themselves!*

Jon had his opinion of which crew members were technically competent and who would need direct supervision when it came to complex problems. He knew who was reliable and who was known to take an extra-long lunch or skip out early. Those who gamed the system or lacked what Jon considered a strong work ethic would lose favor in his eyes.

But in other ways, "not much will change," he explained to his brother one night over celebratory beers. "I'm going to keep working side by side with the crews," he explained. "Otherwise, we'll get too far behind."

Jon's devotion to his friends on the crews ran deep. The more he thought about it, the more he didn't want to risk his relationships with them. He worried, *I don't want to upset the guys, but I also don't want to lose respect. How will I keep everyone happy and still make sure everything gets done?*

He decided to reach out for some advice. He first turned to his dad, who told him, "You can't keep everyone happy. You must be the boss and let everyone know, right off the bat, who's boss. Otherwise, people will walk all over you. If you give people an inch, they'll take a yard."

His friend, Artie, the owner of several auto glass replacement shops, offered slightly different advice. "No one taught me about what it meant to be a boss," he confided. "I wish I'd had someone to tell me that it's a lot harder than it looks. People don't mean it, but they can drive you crazy because sometimes they're reliable and sometimes they're not."

"So, what do you do?" Jon asked, viewing the conversation as a potential crash course in leadership.

"Well, I haven't figured that out!" Artie confessed. "I've had to let some people go because they just couldn't deliver the quality of work I needed. And that's hard to do. I wasn't prepared for how disappointed I would be a lot of the time. I mean, most of the people I hire are decent folks, but I have to keep a tight rein on them."

Jon also picked the brain of Lisa, an analyst in the HR department, as she helped him with paperwork related to his promotion. "I don't think you can be both," she said, in response to his question about how to balance being friends with the people you supervise.

"It's hard sometimes making that transition from coworker to supervisor," she explained, "but it's necessary, because your role is different. You can't give the impression that you favor one employee over another. Most supervisors and managers find it's best to keep a bit of professional distance. It can be difficult to hold your friends accountable, or make decisions on behalf of the organization, if you haven't made that separation."

Jon feigned a quick smile but didn't think her advice was practical. He believed he could maintain his friendships and still be a fair boss.

"You might want to consider taking some classes to help you understand your new responsibilities," she offered. "I can send you information about our upcoming leadership program if you'd like."

He thanked her and told her to feel free to send him the information, but he didn't much care for workshops and programs so he knew he wouldn't take her up on the offer. He really wanted to ask Stu for advice, but if he did, would Stu think he didn't know what he was doing or wonder if he made the right choice selecting Jon instead of Emile? He decided to forego asking Stu for any guidance.

On the Friday before Jon stepped into his new position, however, Stu broached the topic, asking him, "How are you feeling? You ready for this?"

Jon feigned confidence and replied with a quick, "Feeling great! I know just what to do, after all. I had a great mentor." It wasn't a fib. Jon truly looked up to Stu and hoped he could be as good a leader as Stu. He secretly wondered if Stu felt the same amount of insecurity as Jon did when he was a new supervisor. Not wanting to let the opportunity escape, Jon managed a brief "any advice for me?"

"Loads," Stu replied, smiling wryly, "but I'm not so sure how much of it will be helpful. I know you're going to do a great job, Jon. Just remember, you're no longer one of the guys. Your job is to coordinate the work of four crews, and some days you'll feel as though you're on a roller coaster with no way off. Just keep the crews focused, and don't try to do too much. Remember what your purpose and role as a leader is, and you'll do just fine."

Great, Jon wondered, *and what exactly is my role?* He felt a pang of panic as he realized he didn't understand what Stu meant. But instead of asking for clarification, he closed their conversation with a confident "you got it."

In the end, he decided his dad's advice, followed by Artie's, was probably the most practical for him. He would keep a tight leash on the problem guys. He didn't have to worry as much about his friends on the crew; he could trust that they knew what they were doing. That way, he could keep his friendships and still solve some of the problems plaguing the team.

Every Wednesday morning was the regular team meeting, and Jon saw no reason to change this schedule. Normally talkative, Jon was a little nervous to run his first meeting as the new supervisor. Everyone settled in their seats.

"So," he began shyly, "so, I know most of you—some of you real well. And most of you know me. You know what I stand for. You know what you can expect from me. And as far as I'm concerned, with me as the new boss, nothing is really going to change. What I want for us and this team is to help each other out and do good work. And you all know that I have your backs. So, you all have your assignments for the week, but I want to talk to Emile and Joey. Jimmy and Carlos, hang back too, OK?"

A few crew members—some he wasn't expecting—came up to him to shake his hand and offer words of encouragement. "Thanks. Thanks a lot," he replied, giving a signal to his crew leads, Emile and the others, that he would be with them shortly. He thanked his well-wishers, then turned his attention back to his leads. There was a complaint about low water pressure in a residential neighborhood that Emile's team would be investigating, and Jon let him know that he would join them shortly. Joey's crew was laying pipe on a construction site, and Jimmy's team was conducting scheduled pipe replacements. Carlos's team drew the short stick and was handling equipment maintenance and inventory.

"Overall?" He was responding to Stu, who had arrived at the tail end of the meeting. "I think it went fine. I think people know I know my stuff," Jon reflected, as if to himself, as he and Stu walked back to the admin office.

"As long as everyone shows up, follows orders, and does a good job," Jon explained, "we'll be fine."

Jon wanted to be involved in what his crews were doing, and his plan was to work side by side with them. As long as he was there with them, they would be productive, so he planned to spend as much time with the crews as he could.

The two chatted casually before parting ways. Jon didn't stay long in his new office, but instead grabbed his hard hat and his keys and set off to meet Emile's crew. He waved to the receptionist as he headed out of the building, eager to begin his new role as supervisor for maintenance field crews at Axion.

THE QUIET OUTSIDER

Unlike Jon, Avery Daniels was brand new to Axion and the municipal environment. As a CPA with a degree in business, she brought years of accounting, auditing, and payroll experience to her new role at the utility. She was considered a go-to person at her old job. Smart and savvy, Avery was a dependable and hard worker who kept her head down and got things done. She led numerous project teams, but this would be her first formal leadership position.

She first heard about the accounting manager position while working as a consultant to Axion. She was brought in as part of an auditing team to evaluate Axion's books, and over the course of that assignment, Avery quickly became familiar with the organization's technology and procedures. This new position would mean a substantial promotion, more security, and a pathway to more opportunity down the road. When she got the phone call offering her the job, she was ecstatic, but nervous.

She was nervous because the position at Axion put her in charge of eight employees, including accountants, payroll clerks, billing analysts, and collection clerks. Her department provided an array of functions including customer analysis, payment processing, internal accounting, and payroll. Her team of analysts assessed and evaluated usage patterns for both residential and corporate customers. Her accountants handled internal bookkeeping, and her billing analysts dealt with a wide assortment of customer needs including creating payment arrangements for delinquencies. Avery knew that robust systems were in place so everything functioned like a big, simple clock. She wasn't being brought in to innovate because Axion, unlike her previous employer, wasn't about profits, new acquisitions, competitive sales, and innovative product designs. Instead, her new role would be about maintaining the status quo.

She wasn't worried about the technical side of things. Instead, her concern was about the people part. Avery wasn't much of a talker and preferred to work alone. She knew she would have to be a bit more outgoing in this new role, but she hoped not much more. It wasn't that Avery didn't like people. She liked people very much. "Just not every day," she was known to joke.

During the interview, Avery was asked to describe her leadership philosophy. She hadn't really thought much about it before. She figured her job was to oversee the employees and make sure they're doing what they're supposed to do, but beyond that? *It's numbers. We're accountants. There's not a lot that can go wrong,* she reasoned.

In terms of role models, she respected her previous boss, Sarah Hunter, and was envious of her style. Sarah was polished and always appeared put together (so not like Avery) and gave her employees the freedom and independence to make their own decisions and "just do their jobs." When Avery considered what she liked about working for Sarah, she realized it was because *she told us what to do and then got out of our way. We all pretty much knew our jobs and knew what to do, so we didn't really need a leader.*

Avery was holding Sarah in the back of her mind as she gave her answer during the interview. "I think I'm a hands-off leader who doesn't get in people's way," she offered up, hoping it was the answer the interviewers wanted.

"That's good," Ken Johannsen, director of Finance, said, explaining that the previous accounting manager "was a bit of a micromanager."

The panel shared some awkward glances with each other at Ken's reveal. "You might say the team could use some looser reigns," he shared.

"Well," Avery responded to Ken and the other panelists, "I'm a pretty low-key person. It would be disrespectful of me to assume that I can come in here and start changing things or making recommendations on how to do things. Unless people prove otherwise, I assume they are skilled in their jobs and don't need a lot of direct supervision." Then at the last minute she added, "I bring a lot of expertise in process-mapping and systems-thinking that I believe will benefit everyone."

Armed with the knowledge that the previous leader was too strict and stifling, Avery felt more comfortable because she didn't want to have to "manage" people. She especially wasn't going to come in and conduct "those annoying teambuilding retreats where you create structures out of spaghetti." She groaned out loud. "They don't need or want me to babysit," she explained to her wife over dinner, as if rehearsing what she was going to say to them at her first opportunity. "They're professionals, and I will treat them as such."

As time quickly neared for Avery's first week at Axion, however, a few doubts ran through her brain. *What am I supposed to be like?* she wondered. *Will people like and respect me? Some of these folks are more experienced than I am; will they do what I ask them to?*

Like Jon, Avery scheduled a "get to know you" meeting during her first week and was surprised to find that the team organized a breakfast potluck in her honor. Introductions went around the room while they sampled breakfast burritos, fresh fruit, and coffee cake. When it was her turn, Avery took the opportunity to share a little about herself ("Sheila and I have been legally married for seven years"), her work style ("I'm a head-down, get-my-work-done sort of person"), and her leadership style, ("My door is always open—unless it's closed"). She hoped they picked up on her kidding tone in the latter statement, but just to make sure, she added, "But seriously, unless and until I hear from you, I'm not going to bug you. You all know what your jobs are and what you're doing."

Part of her laid-back style to leadership stemmed from her intro-verted personality. While she promoted the concept of an open door, she secretly hoped that her staff didn't need to use it very often. She much preferred the tactical work of her job: digging into a complex spreadsheet, figuring out the source of an error message, running reports, and crunching numbers. She especially loved anything to do with process improvements. "I'll take designing a process map over happy hour with the gang any day of the week," she was known to say.

Avery told the group she didn't anticipate any significant changes to occur over the near future, adding that Ken "is very comfortable with the pace and output of our team. He hasn't asked me to introduce any changes or new initiatives."

Finally, she used the opportunity to explain to her new team that she wasn't the touchy-feely type. "I'm not big on team retreats and potlucks and such." She paused then, realizing her faux pas, and tried to backpedal to save the situation. "Don't get me wrong. I love to eat!" she said, desperate to salvage the situation. "I just mean that I'm not the social butterfly type of person, so parties and potlucks, like this one, aren't top-of-mind for me. I certainly enjoy them, though!"

Feeling the energy lift a little, she tried to close out her first meeting with the group by saying, "I'm looking forward to getting to know you all better and working with all of you." Then she added, "And again, thank you so much for this lovely breakfast! It's a wonderful way to start my day."

Avery stayed a bit longer, nervously tearing at a breakfast croissant, while the team continued to visit, but she didn't know the team members yet, and while they were polite to her, she felt like an awkward outsider. She stood and thanked everyone, once again, for the surprise potluck breakfast.

"I guess I should go finish unpacking and get settled in. I'm sure there isn't much that needs my attention right now, but you never know what Ken has planned for me."

She called over her shoulder as she left the room, "Meeting adjourned!" hoping it would send a subtle message for the team to end socializing in favor of starting their day.

She trusted that, over time, the team would come to view her as a fair and easygoing boss, albeit one with high standards. There was no place for mistakes, especially in their field, and in the past, she was known to be exacting of herself and others. It wasn't beyond her to take over a project if she felt it wasn't proceeding swiftly enough or rewrite reports if they weren't written to her standards. Yes, she was a perfectionist, but, she reasoned, *I think it comes with the job. You've got to care about details and things all adding up to one hundred as an accountant.*

Avery scanned the bare, institutional office walls and the simple, brown desk that made up her new office. She was grateful for the large window that brought sunlight into the otherwise dreary space. *Maybe a plant or two,* she noted. She turned on her PC and rearranged her monitor, moving the metal inbox basket to make space for the second monitor she had requested from IT. And so, Avery Daniels stepped into her role as accounting manager in the Financial Services Division of Axion.

Jon and Avery both began their leadership journeys with little insight about leading others and found themselves wondering, *What is my role now? Am I supposed to be tougher and stricter? Can I still be friends with everyone, or do our relationships change? How do I get my employees to do their jobs and do them correctly?*

There are so many examples of different types of leaders: amazing leaders who make it all look so easy, juxtaposed against an equal number of people in leadership positions who blunder through, leaving a trail of wounded people and damaged organizations in the wake. How do we know what qualities to retain and which ones to throw out? Whom do we mimic and whom do we avoid as role models? When there are so many different examples of leadership, it's hard to know which ones to imitate and which ones to ignore.

Jon learned how to lead from his past bosses who used a traditional "command and control" style of leadership. They were tough disciplinarians who were nice enough but expected few questions and more action. Even Stu, everybody's friend at the plant, was strict and direct. His motto was "job first, talk later." As a result of his past experiences, Jon understood leaders to be tough, direct, and "in charge." If it worked for Jon's bosses, and his father, why would he question it? From Jon's perspective, there wasn't a lot of need for the "people stuff" he heard others talking about. His crew dug trenches, replaced pipes, fixed line breaks, and maintained miles and miles of water lines. It was "hard hat work" that didn't require touchy-feely things like coaching, counseling, rewards, or encouragement. The guys would just think him weak if he gave kudos or had a lot of heart-to-heart conversations. *I know these guys and how they would react. They respond best to orders and directions,* he reasoned. But Jon would come to realize that he'd need to add some different tools if he wanted to be fully effective as a leader. In fact, he would learn if he didn't take care of the people side of things, the rest would fall apart!

Avery never really thought about *how* to lead, and in those situations where a team needed a leader, she was usually the one to do more work, more quickly. She was the go-to gal who had all the answers. Her role model, Sarah, made leadership look easy—so easy that Avery never really felt as though she was being *led*, but rather left to do good work in her own way.

"We really didn't need leadership at my last job," she recalled. "We were all self-directed and content to grind the work out. Sarah handled the big-ticket issues, like getting new clients awarded to the team and securing better budgets and looser timelines."

Avery would soon discover that Sarah did provide leadership to her team. In fact, Avery didn't realize it, but Sarah was such an exceptional leader because the team didn't feel as though they needed her. Avery would later come to learn the interpersonal strategies and techniques that leaders like Sarah bring to their role and just how powerful that approach can be.

As she and Jon would soon discover, effective leadership requires much more than simply having all the answers or being an extra hand on the team. How leaders interact with their team is far more important than anything else. Avery and Jon will both learn they need to do different work as a leader, not more work.

What, in your opinion, are some of the assumptions Jon and Avery hold about what it means to be in a leadership position? What impact will these beliefs have on their ability to lead a team and influence others?

Making the transition from employee to leader is often tricky, especially for someone like Jon who has come up through the ranks and is now supervising his colleagues. What impact do you think it will have on the team if Jon remains friends with some and not others?

Jon and Avery are drawing upon what they've learned from their role models, e.g., previous supervisors and bosses. Who are your leadership role models? In what ways do you model yourself after these individuals?

How would you evaluate Jon's and Avery's first week on the job? What are they doing well? What, in your opinion, could they do differently, and why?

chapter 2

FIGURING OUT YOUR ROLE
AS A SUPERVISOR

"HEY BOSS, HERE ARE THE RESULTS from last week's payroll run. After you review them, they typically go up to Ken." One of her payroll clerks, Lindsay, slid a packet across Avery's desk.

"OK, thanks," Avery sighed, barely looking up from her work. "Just set them on top of the rest."

"Wait, before you go," Avery called out to Lindsay, "I was looking over those personnel action forms, and it looks like there were several terminations that were miscoded. Be really careful with that up front so we don't waste so much time redoing the payroll runs."

"Oh, sure. I'm not sure how that happened, but I'll let them know. Sorry about that," Lindsay said.

"No problem," Avery offered, "but just to make sure, let me review the next few sets before they're entered. I just want to double-check them, OK?"

"Sure," Lindsay answered.

It was a Wednesday, midmorning, and Avery was knee-deep in time-sensitive reports she needed to complete so she could attend a full-day leadership program the following week. She was rummaging through her in-basket, trying to triage items to complete by the end of the day. Her once-bare office was now made a bit homier with several plants; a few pictures; and lots more paperwork, books, and manila folders.

Dennis knocked on her door.

"Got a sec?" he asked.

"You bet. What's up?" Avery looked up but didn't yet turn away from her keyboard.

"Well, I'm trying to confirm the details for next Friday's employee recognition event."

Avery looked up from her work and gave him a visible scowl of disapproval.

"I know, I know," he consoled. Everyone learned early on that Avery wasn't a big fan of office parties. "The caterer just sent me an email with a very different quote than what I was expecting. It's three times what we budgeted for. They said they told me there was a minimum of 500 people to get the reduced rate, but I don't remember ever hearing that, and I'm not seeing that in any email. I don't know what to tell them."

"Are you kidding me?" Avery said, turning her chair to face Dennis squarely. "Well, there's no way we can afford that. Send me the email, and I'll talk to them."

"Thanks!" Dennis said, as he turned on his heels.

Ugh! How did I end up as party planner? she sighed.

Several weeks had passed since Avery began working at Axion, and she was settling comfortably into her new position. She liked the people she worked with and especially liked her boss, Ken. It was an easygoing, laid-back culture at Axion, a sharp contrast to the cutthroat and competitive culture of her previous workplace. At Axion, she found everyone welcoming and nonjudgmental. This made Avery feel more comfortable speaking up in meetings, although she rarely did, and voicing her opinion to staff, which she was beginning to do more and more.

Her biggest challenge was the mountain of paperwork and administrative red tape. (Dot this 'i' but not that one; make sure this gets signed; don't forget to submit this by the end of the week.) For someone who appreciated rules and systems, Avery was surprised how irked she was by the many different procedures she was expected to follow. Already behind on end-of-month reports, she had vendor proposals to review for an impending performance management software upgrade. The previous manager had supposedly begun the review, but Avery had yet to find any evidence of that work.

Avery was learning more and more about her team and found them technically competent. However, she noticed a continuous pattern of simple mistakes in payroll and billing—for example, miscoding pay rates. The perfectionist in her was easily irritated by *such sloppy work*, and Avery found herself devoting more time to reviewing her clerks' work to circumvent errors. *On top of everything else I have to get done,* she found herself thinking, *I also have to check everyone's work?*

She assumed things would smooth out once she got a handle on their processes and could properly assess training needs for the staff. Many of the procedures in her department were clunky, with layers of approvals that just begged for simplification. She smiled to herself: *Maybe some cool, new process maps might be in order.*

Newly energized, she powered through a couple of the easier items on her to-do list, then devoted some time to scratch out some process maps on her new whiteboard. It wasn't until Dennis waved a goodbye, passing her office, that she realized it was quitting time. Seeing him reminded her about the discrepancy with the caterers for next week's employee event.

Dang! I forgot. She wrote a sticky note reminder to "call caterers" and placed it in the center of her monitor.

"I guess that's about all I can do for today," she announced out loud, to no one in particular. She glanced at her desk and the list of items that still needed her attention:

- a month-end payroll report to review
- two memos to draft
- several invoices to approve
- four requisitions to approve
- two leave requests from staff
- a note from the IT director, disputing a recent payroll adjustment
- a request from her boss, Ken, to review proposals from three new software vendors and submit her recommendations to the advisory team working on the performance management software upgrade

I'll jump on those proposal reviews for Ken tomorrow, she promised herself. What Avery didn't realize was that some of the items in her inbox were more pressing than Ken's research project, and a backlog was beginning to form.

THE COMPLAINT DEPARTMENT

The shift from Joan, the previous supervisor, to Avery was proving a hard transition for Lindsay. Lindsay had been led to think that Joan was a micromanager, but Avery put Joan to shame.

"It's going to really slow us down," Lindsay complained, with a cautionary tone. She was spending lunch with one of her colleagues from another department and sharing her frustrations about Avery. "I don't think she realizes the impact she's having. We used to be able to run our own payroll reports and fix our own errors. But if I have to wait for her to review my work and then make corrections? It's going to really slow us all down. I mean, I thought she was all 'Just do your job, and I won't bug you.'"

"Don't get me wrong," she continued, "She's a really nice woman," emphasizing the word "really." "It's just that she doesn't know how to manage."

"What is it that she does or doesn't do?" her friend, Shelly, asked.

"Well, for one thing, she can't make a decision to save her life," Lindsay explained. "She sits on things for a really long time. And this need to review everything is just tedious. I really don't know why she has us here, because she basically does everything herself."

Lindsay liked her freedom to manage her own schedule and work at her own pace, but because Avery was conducting oversight of her work, she was feeling smothered.

On those occasions when she asked Avery a question, Avery wasn't very quick to respond. Lindsay submitted a request as early as possible to attend a vendor conference on software upgrades, but despite her reminder emails, she never heard back from Avery, so she couldn't attend.

Lindsay described the incident with the conference as something that "wasn't really that big of a deal. Disappointing, yes, but I understand how things can get lost in the shuffle." But there were several other circumstances when Avery's slow response made Lindsay look unprofessional and incompetent. "I really don't care what her decision is," she told Shelly. "Just tell me so I can move on with my work."

Avery's indecision didn't merely affect Lindsay. It was also impacting other departments that needed answers from her. Lindsay's frustration was apparent. "I've been doing this for a long time," Lindsay said. "I know what I'm doing."

"Well," she said, bringing her rant to a close, "I guess we'll see what new procedures the new boss decides to implement at our next staff meeting. *If* we have one, that is." Lindsay and Shelly packed up their lunch items and headed back to their respective offices.

A CREW OF ONE: 24/7, 365 DAYS/YEAR

"What people need to know about me," Jon announced loudly to a group of colleagues over lunch, "is I am all-in for my guys. They know I have their backs, and they have mine!" It had been several weeks, and Jon was proud of how well things were going. Sure, there were a few challenges, but nothing Jon couldn't handle. He enjoyed being the go-to person for crew members and helping them out whenever he could. "It's nice to know that all of this knowledge," he tapped his forefinger on his temple, "isn't going to waste."

One afternoon, he arrived at a job site and noticed the crew struggling with what should have been a quick fix. "Whoa," he interjected, moving quickly to the team. "That's not cool, you guys. Make sure that doesn't touch the ground. We don't want any contamination."

Jon enjoyed sharing his knowledge and teaching his crew. "No one told me these things; I had to figure them out on my own," he explained one afternoon after demonstrating a shortcut for placing a repair clamp on a length of pipe. "You guys are so lucky you got me as a boss," he told them, only partially joking.

If he anticipated a potential problem, he was quick to offer guidance. "If anything goes wrong, it's my butt on the line, not theirs," he was known to explain to anyone who would listen. "And if anything were to happen to any of them, it's also on me."

Just the day before, Jon had arrived at a water break and eagerly jumped into action, directing crew members to dig at a location he designated. "I would extend that farther out," he directed. He continued to instruct, barely pausing between orders. "Jimmy, get on the horn and see who we've got to help with excavation." With Jon on site, Jimmy was relegated to worker, his expertise not needed. The others stood by, waiting for direction.

It doesn't make sense for my crew to struggle, especially if I already know the answer. My job is to help us be more efficient and get more done, he reasoned.

Jon told others he didn't want to be one of those bosses who was "out of touch," and that no job was too big or too small for him. But in reality, he didn't want to be out of the loop. He wanted to maintain control and know what was happening at all times. He figured if he was helping, he could stay on top of things.

Another crew jumped into action when they saw his truck arrive on site. *They should already have their locates*, he wondered, *so why are they hangin' out, goofing off, and looking like deadbeats?* He chastised them about appearing idle to the public. "I don't need people thinking that my guys are just hangin' out, wasting time," he barked. He was rattled by what he assumed was laziness.

Jon confessed his frustration to Stu at the end of a particularly stressful week. Several employees had called in sick, which made two crews shorthanded. "I'm glad I can answer their questions and help them out," he told Stu, "but I don't see them taking a lot of initiative, you know? They just sort of wait around until I tell them what to do. I was never like that. I don't get that attitude."

"It does seem like you're running circles around everyone," Stu said. "And, even so, I'm not seeing the speed that we need on some of these job sites," he cautioned.

"It sometimes feels like they're doing it on purpose, to bug me. Like they know what to do, but they don't do it, you know?" He jokingly told Stu, "It isn't much of an exaggeration anymore. I really am working 24/7, 365 days a year."

Stu wasn't laughing. "Well, I think we've got enough guys who can help take some of the load off so you're not working 24/7, 365," he said.

Truthfully, Stu wasn't giving Jon the full picture. He was getting earfuls from crew members about Jon's controlling style. Jon's crews were underperforming compared to other teams doing similar work. The common denominator was Jon. Stu knew Jon was having a hard time letting go of some of the tasks he used to do and decisions he used to make, but he wanted to give him the opportunity to turn things around on his own. Concerned Jon needed more guidance, Stu tried a little subtle prodding.

"I'm wondering if you're doing too much, Jon. Maybe you need to start to delegate a bit more," he suggested.

"No way," Jon stated. "How can I let them do more if they don't know what to do? They're not showing me they know their stuff. Until they do, I'll just keep on 'em." Jon was determined to figure out a way to motivate his crews so they would work faster, harder, and smarter.

"Jon," Stu frowned, then stated in a tone that would make Jon listen, "I brought you on to lead the work, not do the work."

Stu made his next move. "There's a leadership program that's being offered, and I think you'd get a lot out of it. It meets monthly. First session starts next Wednesday. I'd like for you to sign up and attend."

"We have way too much going on for me to go to training. That'll level me," Jon protested.

"It might take you away for a few days, but I think you'll benefit in the long run. I'll email you the link to sign up when I get back to my desk." Stu gave him a reassuring pat on the back, then clarified, "It's not a suggestion."

As soon as Jon arrived back to his office, there was an email from Stu with the link to register for the Moving into Leadership program. After a few clicks, he was scheduled for the first session on the following Wednesday.

Jon looked at the piles of papers on the corner of his desk, reached in his top drawer for one of the energy bars he stashed, and shrugged. *Who knows?* he pondered. *Maybe it'll help me motivate these guys.*

for your consideration

What are some of the challenges Jon and Avery are facing as they integrate into their new roles?

Avery seems to be getting overwhelmed with tasks and responsibilities. How is this affecting her relationship with Lindsay and other team members?

Jon has valiantly stepped up to help out his crews, but how do you think his involvement with the crews will impact his relationship with his employees? How will his involvement affect the crews' productivity and morale?

What's your assessment of how Jon and Avery are transitioning into their roles as leaders? Give some examples of positive decisions each has made so far and choices you believe were misguided.

chapter 3

SELF-AWARENESS AND LEADERSHIP STYLE

JON WAS LESS THAN EAGER TO ATTEND the leadership training Stu and Lisa, from HR, promoted. "I'm just not a 'college guy,'" he claimed, hoping Stu would agree and release him from the obligation. "And I can't help us get caught up if I'm stuck in a class."

Stu remained steadfast. "If you keep an open mind," he suggested, "you might find it worth your time."

Jon grumbled under his breath as he walked to the administration building where training sessions were conducted. *Six sessions?* He was shocked to discover what he had agreed to by clicking that link sent by Stu. *They're expecting me to take off a full day every month? That's crazy!* he complained.

At his morning meeting, he informed the crews he would be in a class for the day. "But I'm available by text if you have any questions—any questions at all. Call if it's urgent." He was looking straight at Joey, one of his crew leads who Jon recently found the need to supervise more closely. He instructed his crew leads to check in with him every two hours with updates. As he left, he gave other crew members reminders to "don't forget …" and "make sure you …." It was a busy week, and the day could easily unravel without his oversight, but he didn't have a choice. If necessary, he could always step out for a few hours. Stu didn't need to know.

The workshop began on a worse note than Jon expected. After introducing herself, the facilitator then asked the group to introduce themselves. "Tell us something unique about you—something that your colleagues don't already know about you."

"Everybody here …," Jon said, "they all know me."

Jon wasn't much for formalities, so he was edgy about the length of time spent on introductions and niceties. *Get to the point,* he urged silently, hoping to hasten the program along.

"There is no one way to lead, and there is no magic mushroom you can take to guide you in your decisions," said the facilitator. "The best place for us to begin is with ourselves," she continued. "You are a unique individual with unique talents, qualities, and even quirks as a leader. The most effective leaders are highly aware of their strengths and draw upon them when leading others. In this program, we'll conduct several different assessments that will help you learn more about yourself. The reason it's so important for you to know yourself is because, when you're in a leadership position, you're highly visible. Part of being an effective leader is understanding your personality style and how you come across to others."

She continued, "You'll lose credibility with others if you're trying to be someone you're not. It doesn't take long for others to come to understand you and your strengths and weaknesses. I believe there are specific responsibilities when leading a team, which we'll talk about in this program, but how you do these things is distinct to you.

"Imagine this," she said. "You arrive here at work, saying 'good morning' to colleagues and coworkers as you arrive. Then, you turn the corner and encounter your boss. What sort of greeting do you receive from your boss? Is your boss happy to see you? Does your boss seem happy to be at work and eager to begin the day? Or does your boss seem a little grumpy and walk right past you without looking you in the eye or saying 'hello'? What sort of impact does that interaction with the boss have on you?

"Now imagine that you've encountered yourself: You're the boss! What's it like to work for you? What image do you think you project?"

With an invitation to the participants, they began to jot down their thoughts and ideas in the journals they were provided.

"Do you seek to create a positive tone, arriving to work on time and ready to go? Or do you slink into your office without speaking to anyone, holding tight to your coffee until you wake up and feel ready to talk to others?"

The facilitator paused to allow them to continue writing.

"Are you aware of the messages your actions send to the rest of your team?" she asked. And then, "Here's an interesting one: Are you eager to discuss issues, give constructive feedback, and take constructive feedback? Do you offer praise and encouragement when warranted and keep the group focused when necessary? Do you gripe about new initiatives or complain about having to attend meetings? Or is your message one of energy and commitment to the work at hand?"

The class seemed engrossed in their own thoughts, and many people continued to write.

"As a leader, you set the tone for your team. Your mood, your habits, your attitudes, and your perspectives become guideposts for the team. If you were a fly on the wall for a day, observing your interactions with members of your team, what would you notice about how you:

- give out assignments
- provide feedback
- reward good work
- handle last-minute changes
- address problems
- Take your time with your answers."

The participants continued to write their ideas in response to her questions.

"What would you observe about what it's like to:

- Meet with you, one-on-one? If I report to you, what do we discuss in our meetings together, and how do you make me feel? Motivated? Secure? Encouraged? Excited to tackle the work? Do I feel as though I can come back and ask questions if I'm uncertain or if I encounter a glitch?
- Participate in a team meeting. Are your team meetings productive, or does the team hash out the same things week after week? Does everyone engage in lively discussions and debate? Or are decisions the result of a few team members who dominate the discussions? What's it like to be a voice of dissent on your team? Does it feel risky to speak up and share a contrary

opinion? Or are diverse opinions and ideas valued on your team? Do you thank people for sharing different perspectives and ask for opinions and ideas? Who leads team meetings? Is it usually you who creates the meeting agendas, runs the meetings, and does most of the talking? Or are these responsibilities shared? Can team members:

- admit a mistake to you?
- bring new ideas to you?
- ask for help?
- tell you they don't agree?

"As the leader of a team, you must be conscious and intentional about everything you do, because your team members will take their lead from you about how we do things around here," the facilitator stated.

"When you step into any sort of leadership position, you're on stage. Think fishbowl. If you're cynical about the direction your organization is moving or are struggling to find meaning in the work you do, you may unintentionally be putting off a vibe that says, 'I'm not happy.' It's difficult to expect enthusiasm and commitment from those you supervise if they don't see it from you, their leader. But if you're excited about your work, show up with purpose, and have a positive attitude, it will infect your team."

The deep, personal reflection the facilitator was asking of participants was making Jon nervous. "Is this a counseling session or a class?" Jon said out loud to the classmate on his right. None of this seemed relevant to the problems he was facing with his crew. He needed help with getting people motivated. *They don't need to know what kind of leader I am, just that I **am** their leader,* he thought.

Feeling anxious and a little bored, Jon flipped over his phone and began to text Emile, who was checking on a water pressure complaint. Dissatisfied with his response, Jon left the room so he could talk by phone.

When he returned, the facilitator was introducing the next activity. Jon joined his group, but barely participated. Activities and games, he felt, were beneath his stature as a supervisor. *Just give me information,* he thought, *and quit wasting my time with these silly activities.* The class was lively and talkative, and Jon did his best to look interested, but his phone and his email account beckoned.

"In my experience," the facilitator offered, as the group members closed out their discussion, "it's never worked when I've tried to be leaderlike. It's always come across as phony and contrived. It's often tempting to try to mask or disguise what you don't know to convince others you're the right pick for the job. But guard against the urge to do this. For one thing, you won't be able to pretend to be someone you're not for very long. Effective leaders know what they're good at, and they don't waste time or energy trying to be someone or something they're not."

Jon was tuned out during this portion of the facilitator's monologue, as he had just received an email from Jimmy. As he typed his response, the facilitator continued. "You're leading a team, and each member—including you—brings something unique to the team. Take a genuine interest in the talents, skills, knowledge, and experiences that your team members bring, and surround yourself with that talent. Think of your team as an orchestra. When everyone brings their best, you can create beautiful results! Your role is to facilitate the movement and interplay of all the various team members, so they create a cohesive sound."

Jon lifted his head when he heard the reference to orchestra. "More like a high school marching band," he smirked.

"When you step into a leadership position, the focus is less about you and more about what others need from you so they can succeed. Let's take a short break, and when we return, we'll continue this discussion. Come back, please, at ten fifteen. Thank you."

As Jon started to leave for his break, the facilitator approached him. "I've noticed you taking numerous calls this morning, Jon. Do you have someone who can take over for you when you're in a training class like this one?"

"No one," he answered sternly. "No one can!" Jon continued, getting a little exasperated. "You need to understand that, as supervisor, I work 24/7, 365 days a year. Unlike some of the others in this room, I am on call at all times. If my boss emails or calls me, I need to respond immediately. I'm in charge of several large crews of people who need me."

"I see," said the facilitator. "Well, I'm even more appreciative that you're balancing your responsibilities with attending this workshop. That sounds like a tricky balancing act."

Jon mumbled a short "you have no idea" under his breath as left the room to seek out something to drink. He was annoyed that he had to take so much time away from his real work to attend a training that had, so far, offered him little practical advice he could implement.

So far, all we've talked about is ourselves! What a waste of time, he thought, and then out loud, to no one in particular, he expressed his frustration, "I feel like I'm doing the job of four people. How about teaching me how to get lazy people motivated, or make sure people show up on time, or don't take long lunches, or goof off?" He looked around the break room to see if anyone had heard him.

Their break over, the facilitator called the room back to order with a question.

"Now that we better understand ourselves, how do you think your team would describe your style as a leader?"

It might have been an interesting question, but Jon was distracted by all the pressing concerns of his day. He thought about his reputation in the field and how he was known as a hard worker and someone who was trustworthy and reliable. He could outwork anyone on his team. And he was loyal, too. He was always the first to arrive at work and often the last to leave. No one at Axion could doubt his dedication to the job.

Many of the participants in the class were sharing similar ideas about themselves. Dedicated. Honest. Loyal. Committed. Hard workers. Competent.

"These are noble characteristics—all of them," the facilitator commented. "But what do they say about your leadership style? In other words, those qualities will color the way in which you lead a team."

Jon was now tuning back into the conversation, and his facial expression didn't hide his confusion. Others in the room looked around nervously, too. One class member finally broke the silence, "What do you mean?"

"For example, if you're a particularly driven individual, it will show up in how you interact with your team. Your team members may think they're expected to work as long and hard as you do. That may not be your intention, but it may come across to others." She paused, then continued, "Or, for example, if you're a very focused or structured person, your team will come to rely on structure, guidelines, and systems from you.

"If you're intuitive about others," she went on, "you probably connect easily to others on a personal or emotional level. Your team members will come to expect open dialogue, frank conversations, and communication from you. See what I mean?"

Avery, who had been listening intently, took this occasion to finally speak up and offer an example. "Well, I'm pretty detail-oriented. I have to be, in my work as an accountant. But what does that have to do with my leadership style?" she asked.

The facilitator turned the question around to the class. "Let's ask the group. If Avery was your boss, what are some possible ways her attention to detail might show up when she interacts with you?"

"Well, does she scrutinize my work? If so, I'd probably think she was a nitpicker," came one response. There was some laughter from the group.

"That would drive me crazy!" came another.

"Yes, and what is the value that her attention to detail could possibly bring to her team?" Hearing no answers, the facilitator pressed. "Think about it." She waited, giving the group time to think.

"I suppose it depends on the kind of work we do," came one response. "In accounting, that's probably important. In maintenance, maybe not so much, and it might make me feel like she doesn't see me and my contributions if she's only focused on the little details."

Another new supervisor shared her thought. "I think it's important to have someone care about the details, especially if they're important to the work we do."

"As you gain more awareness about your personality traits," the facilitator explained, "it's helpful to communicate and educate your staff about your style. Your staff members need to understand where you come from and how that impacts them. For example, your message to them might be, 'While I'm a stickler for details, it's because I'm passionate about meeting goals. You can count on me to push us all to success.'"

Avery laughed out loud. "I probably should be paying attention to details for that reason! I'm not so sure that's my true motivation, but it probably should be, huh?"

The facilitator smiled, and light laughter broke out across the room. One participant shared, "I would hope if Avery was my boss, she would let me know that she focuses on the details to help us as a team."

"It's true. I can get lost in the minutia and forget that others aren't as obsessed about details as I am," Avery admitted.

The facilitator continued to give examples of how to translate personal style, preferences, and talents into leadership strengths, and therefore, value for the team.

"If you're very driven and push yourself, will you drive your team as well? You have to know that your challenge is knowing when to back off and give folks a break," the facilitator said. "Your team members will want to know that you recognize this. Let them know, 'I'll push us hard, but I also know when it's time to celebrate our accomplishments.'

"How might your employees perceive those of you who are shy, quiet, and introverted and prefer working quietly all day at your desk?" she asked.

"That's me!" one person shouted out, admitting his preference. "They probably wonder what I do all day and say, 'He's always hidden away in his office. Or he's never available.'"

"Yes, if you consider yourself to be quiet and shy," the facilitator continued, "be open to the fact that some of your team members might interpret your need for solitude to mean that you're unapproachable. As a result, they may not come to you as often as they want to, or need to, for questions, input, or counsel."

"So how can you address their concerns?" came a question to the room.

"Well," Avery spoke up again, "I told my group right away, 'My door is always open, unless it's closed.'" She paused, then continued, "But what I was really trying to say is, 'I may not always look like it, but I always have time for each of you.'"

The facilitator encouraged the class to break into small groups and discuss how their personalities might be interpreted differently by their teams, and how their preferences might create challenges for their teams.

Finally, the facilitator began to bring the discussion to a close before lunch. She made one final point, which she said was most important.

"While it's important to use your strengths and talents when leading a team, it doesn't let you off the hook for doing things that don't come naturally." She paused, to take in how the group responded to this. "For example, you may not necessarily like to give feedback, or deal with conflict, or give praise. But when leading a team, you'll be expected to do these and many other things that may not be in your comfort zone."

She encouraged participants to identify skills or areas that might challenge them, whether face-to-face communication, dealing with workplace conflict, problem-solving, or decision-making.

"We all have weak areas," she explained, "or what I call challenge areas. You don't have to run out and hire a professional coach or sign up immediately for a class. But you do need to be aware of your weaknesses and let others know that you're aware of them, too. We want to be role models for our employees. If you don't seek out opportunities to learn new skills or improve, how can you expect your team members to do so?"

The class stirred restlessly on the heels of that comment. Sensing the shift in energy, the facilitator brought the morning session to a close. "With that, let's break for lunch, and when we return, you'll receive your custom personality profiles and we'll do more work around this topic of self-awareness. Have a nice lunch, and I'll see you back here at one o'clock."

When the class filed back in from lunch, the facilitator announced that the group would be reviewing the results of their personality assessments. Prior to the first workshop, each participant completed an online questionnaire designed to assess their thinking preferences, decision-making styles, and behavioral tendencies.

"As you can imagine, there are many tools or assessments that can help you better understand your personality style, how you deal with conflict, your strengths, your decision-making style, and many other aspects about yourself. By now, you've probably encountered one or two of these instruments in your career. Axion prefers Emergenetics©[1], so that's the instrument we're using for this program. But there are many other instruments out there, such as:

- DISC
- StrengthsFinder
- Meyers-Briggs Type Indicator (MBTI)
- Insights Discovery
- True Colors
- Keirsey Temperament SorterThomas-Kilmann Conflict Mode Instrument

Jon entered the class, late, talking on his phone.

"Whichever personality assessment or psychometric tool you use," the facilitator said, nodding to Jon, still on his phone, "the important thing to remember is to use it! These instruments don't do us any good if they're locked in a drawer. For the remainder of the afternoon, we'll dive a bit deeper into your unique preferences and how your personality influences your leadership style."

After Jon received his profile, he found it interesting, but it made little impact on him. He failed to see how the results of his questionnaire, depicted in a colorful pie chart, would help him motivate his blue-collar workers who were more interested in the paycheck and salary increases than kudos and time off. He wanted to know what to say or not say to keep them on track, loyal, and focused on the job. "All the rest," he muttered to himself, "is just colored pictures."

Avery, on the other hand, was fascinated by the results of her profile. Seeing that her preference was to analyze and organize made sense to her. It explained why she liked nothing better than to analyze a spreadsheet and find errors. Sometimes she would spend hours researching and analyzing a complicated field of data until she could finally announce, like Sherlock Holmes might, "Aha! I've got it!" She was energized by creating systems and procedures. Process maps, agile thinking, Six Sigma—all the tools to keep her focused, on time, and productive—were indicative of how she thinks and solves problems, just as her personality profile revealed.

Now I understand how my need to deeply analyze things slows down my decision-making. It's no wonder I can spend hours deliberating on a decision! And then she acknowledged, *"that probably drives some of my staff crazy."*

The results from her personality profile also illustrated why tasks, and not relationships, motivated her. "I like people," she repeated her signature joke to the people in her small group, in her typical deadpan manner, "just not every day."

The afternoon consisted of activities and small-group discussions, which seemed irrelevant and childish to Jon. Throughout the afternoon, Jon stayed glued to his phone, leaving regularly to take calls. Despite the fact he was stuck in this class, he rationalized, *at least I can keep tabs on everybody. Gotta love modern technology.*

He was reading an email from Jimmy when he heard, "I look forward to seeing you all again next month." He barely took the time to gather his things before speeding from the room. He was exhausted from playing two roles today. Avery, too, was exhausted from a day of introspection, reflection, and discussion that was especially tiring for an introvert like her. She left the classroom, eager for some well-deserved downtime at home.

Self-awareness is arguably the most important aspect of effective leadership. Highly effective leaders know their strengths, passions, and talents and are equally in tune with their challenge areas (or weaknesses), hot buttons, and quirks so they can manage them when necessary. As you read this story about Avery and Jon, what are you noticing about their personalities and how their personalities impact their leadership style?

Why do you think it's important for leaders to have a high level of self-awareness?

How would you describe yourself as a leader? What strengths and abilities do you bring as a leader? What are some of your personal challenge areas? How will your strengths and weaknesses impact your influence as a leader?

How will you describe yourself and your leadership style to your staff? Is your perception of your leadership style congruent with how others view you?

Finally, if you've completed any sort of personality assessment in the past, now is a great time to find it, review it, and analyze the insights it provides into your leadership style.

chapter 4

MANAGING TIME AND
RESPONSIBILITIES

FROM SUNUP TO SUNDOWN, Jon immersed himself in his new role. He was the first to arrive to work because he wanted to greet crew members and make sure everyone arrived on time. He created a small team of employees to serve as floaters, handling special projects or accompanying him if emergencies arose (which was very often the case). His days were a blur of meetings and visits to job sites. Real lunches were a luxury; he typically grabbed a quick sandwich or energy bar between meetings.

He was also the last to leave. This was not always by design. Every time he returned to his office, he got caught in a web of endless emails that required some sort of response. Some days, it took him hours to reply to these emails, which consisted of vendor inquiries, employee requests, and correspondence on meetings.

It was the throngs of paperwork that caught him by surprise. In the first few weeks of his new position, he had to figure out how to correct a missed shipment from a vendor and approve numerous purchase requisitions for new equipment and employee safety gear. If he had to sign it, he wanted to know what he was signing, so he reviewed every single document, order, and request that left his department.

He corrected timesheets that were then sent to payroll, approved leave requests, and created work schedules, taking requests for vacations and leave into consideration.

Recently, he had to decide between two leave requests for the exact same week. One was from Dillon, a long-term crew member, and the other was submitted by a new employee, Sam, who indicated his mother, in California, was having surgery. Since both were on Jimmy's team, Jon couldn't afford to have both employees off for a full week. Sam's request seemed the most urgent, so Jon approved it, making a mental note to explain his decision to Dillon.

In addition, Jon was required to rearrange workloads when crew members were sick, which seemed to happen more than Jon ever imagined! On average, he began to figure, he had two team members out each week for one illness or another. It seemed a little high to him. He made it a point to pay more attention to what was going on with the crews to determine, he chuckled to himself, if they were truly sick, or just "sick of work." *I can't afford people to be out,* he decided, making another point to inform the crew leads he would be cracking down on unauthorized absences.

He was also surprised by the number of meetings he was asked to attend. As a crew lead, he met only with Stu, discussing project timelines and assignments. But now, as a supervisor, it appeared that his insight was necessary on all sorts of matters, from planning meetings with engineers, to regular updates with Stu, to monthly meetings with all supervisors from the division. In addition, Jon conducted the weekly Wednesday morning meetings with the entire crew and morning operational meetings with crews to discuss specific assignments for the day. All the morning meetings cut into the time he had to prepare for the rest of the day.

Jon found that he sailed through technical decisions, such as scheduling, problem-solving, or overseeing crew work. It was the people-side of things that was taking more energy than he realized. There was always some sort of employee issue going on. "If I didn't have to deal with the people," he told his wife one evening, "the job would be a cinch."

He did what made sense—took his hard hat and went out to the job sites to help out his crews. He believed his help was paying off, as he noticed his crews completing patches and repairs faster than ever before.

"Hey, Jimmy," Jon said, waving to his crew lead as he arrived on a job site one afternoon. But Jon did not like what he saw. The site was littered with tools, and two team members were having a heated argument in their truck. Jimmy and Dillon were working to secure a pipe fitting.

"Hey, Dillon," Jon said, "just wanted to let you know I approved your leave request." Distracted by watching the two work, Jon inadvertently told Dillon he could have the week off.

"Thanks," Dillon said, struggling to open a valve. Jon watched for a few minutes, then approached them. "You know, if you worked from that left side, it might be a bit easier. Let me show you a trick I learned …"

Dillon stepped away from his work as Jon approached. Taking Dillon's wrench, Jon easily opened the valve. Dillon and Jimmy stood behind him, watching as he worked.

"See that?" Jon asked, handing the wrench back to Dillon. "Another thing I always try to do is presoak the bolts with penetrating oil—always use food grade, by the way, just to be safe. It just seems to save time. OK," Jon crossed his arms, surveying the job site a final time, satisfied with his contribution to the scene. "Make sure you get all this cleaned up before you leave," he cautioned, and he started toward his truck.

He motioned to Jimmy to accompany him. "I don't like the way this job site looks, man, with these tools laying around like this. It makes us look sloppy."

"I know it looks bad, but before you got here ..." Jimmy began to explain.

"No excuses," Jon interrupted, taking off his hard hat and tossing it on the passenger side of the truck. He started the engine and drove off, giving Jimmy no opportunity to explain the reason for the messy work site. Jimmy prided himself on his work ethic and didn't much care for how dismissive Jon was toward him.

Jimmy watched him drive off, then turned back to Dillon, "OK, then," he said, feigning a cheery tone, "Where were we?"

The same trend continued as Jon visited the other crews. So many of them were not working efficiently! By the end of the day, Jon was short-tempered and frustrated by what he perceived to be sloppy—and lazy—work. *These guys wouldn't get anything done if I wasn't around,* he griped silently to himself as he arrived back at his office.

Checking his emails, he noticed he was late for a planning meeting with Stu and two engineers in charge of an expansion project. "Damnit!" he cursed, grabbing his notebook and racing down the hallway.

"Sorry I'm late," he said, out of breath as he entered the conference room. "Been putting out fires in the field."

Stu shot him a stern look that said *this is not acceptable*, but actually replied, "Glad you could make it. We were just going over the West-End upgrade. Do you have the schedule for the team you'll be sending to the site?"

Jon sat down quickly, pulling out his notebook. He had completely forgotten about this construction project and was going to have to admit to Stu and the others that he failed to put one of his maintenance teams on the project. "I had a few last-minute leave requests that put a glitch in my schedule," he told the group, "but I think I can get it finalized and to you all by the end of the day tomorrow."

Jon hated to admit it, but he was having a hard time keeping up with his responsibilities. Things were falling through the cracks. *How did Stu do it?* he wondered. There was always so much to do, from meetings, to scheduling employees, to making sure his crews were doing a good job. After a long day of meetings, visiting each job site, and answering employee questions, he had little energy left to devote to his own responsibilities.

Jon wasn't eager for his lashing from Stu, but he stayed after the meeting anyway. "Sorry I was late, boss," he said, with contrition.

"Don't let it keep happening," Stu said, as they walked together to the admin building. "I'm more concerned that your responsibilities are not being met. You're still new at this, so I'm giving you some slack, but managing time is important. Aren't they covering this in the leadership program?"

"Yeah," Jon fibbed. He wasn't sure if time management had been addressed in the program, but he didn't want Stu to think he needed help. He made a mental note to research time management when his phone vibrated with a text from Emile.

"What's up?" Stu asked, seeing the change in Jon's demeanor.

"Break over at the Simco complex," Jon replied.

"Weren't we just over there?" Stu asked, holding the door open for Jon. Jon searched his memory, trying to recall if his crew had been to Simco in the last month. Simco was one of the city's largest industrial customers, and Axion worked hard to maintain good relations with its managers. If there was a break that required even a temporary water shutoff, it would affect not only Simco's operations, but its customers and neighboring businesses, too.

"I don't recall," he replied. Stu and Jon stood in front of the bank of mail slots. Stu skimmed through his small stack of envelopes while he listened to Jon's conversation with Emile. He peppered Emile with questions to assess the situation.

"You got this?" Stu asked.

Jon nodded and gave him a thumbs-up sign. This was what he loved about his job. Always something new happening. He listened to Emile's description of the situation. "Uh-huh," Jon said, "OK, well, go ahead and secure the area. Do we know if that pipe is concrete? No? OK, here's what I want you to do ..."

Emile was standing with two of his crew members at the site of the water main break and had a clear sense of how the repair should be made. Frustrated by Jon's unwillingness to listen to his recommendations, he listened to Jon's directions by phone. "You sure, boss? We're thinking that we can ..."

Jon didn't give him a chance to finish, "I've worked so much pipe over there," he said. "I'm positive."

Jon had made his way back to his office and found another one of Jimmy's crew members, Jay, standing in his doorway.

Jon looked at him, as if to say, "What'cha need?"

"Seems like you're busy; I can come back," Jay said, but Jon cut him off. "On my way to a break," he said, moving the phone away from his mouth. "What 'cha need?"

"I wanted to explain about a leave slip I submitted," Jay said. "It's my daughter's quinceañera, and we're having a bunch of family in," he explained.

"Hold on a minute, Emile," Jon said into the phone.

"Sure, sure," Jon said. "As long as Jimmy's cool with it and you all have the coverage?"

Jay shrugged and offered a meek, "I think so."

"Then I'm sure it'll be fine," Jon said. "On my way," he said, returning to his call with Emile.

"Thanks," Jay replied as he watched Jon head out to meet up with the crew on McPherson Avenue.

By the time Jon arrived at McPherson Avenue, the crews were already filling the hole after fixing the leak.

"That was fast," Jon said.

"We just did what you said," Emile replied. Emile's patience was wearing thin with Jon's dismissive attitude toward him and the other more senior members of the crew. He had far too much experience and expertise to be treated as a rookie.

"If he doesn't want my input, then we'll just do exactly what he says to do— exactly," he recounted to Jimmy later that afternoon. "We'll see how long he can run this show as a crew of one."

A MISSED OPPORTUNITY

"Are we having a team meeting today?" Alice asked, poking her head in Avery's office.

"I don't know; I'm slammed," Avery said. "Do we need one?"

Alice was noncommittal. "It doesn't matter to me. I just thought

I'd check because others were asking me."

"Let's skip it this week," Avery said. "I've really got to get these numbers up to Ken. Will you let everyone know?"

"Sure thing," Alice said. Avery heard Alice's announcements as she moved down the hallway: "No meeting today." "Meeting canceled for today, guys." "No meeting today. Maybe next week."

Avery breathed a sigh of relief. She was grateful for the extra hour she just bought herself, and for the break from having to engage in forced conversation with the team. Their team meetings were painful. "It's like trying to get rocks to talk," she described to her wife one evening. Hardly anyone spoke, and when they did, it was simply to chime in with an empty statement like "nothing new here" or "same as last week." Avery figured it was more productive to hold fewer meetings, so people had more to share. And besides, she got the impression her team loved these meetings about as much as she did. She jotted a reminder to herself to switch team meetings to every other month.

Avery did a little stretch in her chair, then rifled through her inbox, looking for an old email. *Didn't I already put together that software comparison?* she wondered. Ken and the rest of the subcommittee were eager for her recommendations, so she wanted to get her thoughts submitted to the team. *Where is it? I'm pretty sure I put those recommendations together.* She was feeling a sense of panic by the sheer volume of work that was uncompleted. In addition to the software vendor recommendations, she was still reviewing payroll reports and was planning to develop a training for her payroll clerks.

Avery prided herself on being organized and productive, but lately she was drowning in paperwork, emails, and meeting requests. She was missing appointments and falling behind in her work, which was unlike her.

She was distracted by a "ding" signaling an incoming email from the director of Human Resources:

Hi Avery,

Hope this finds you well. I'm putting together a meeting with the subcommittee to review bid proposals for the performance management software. Do you have time this week? Have you and Ken reviewed the finalists that are being proposed for the upgrade?
I can't do next week because I'll be out of town.

Thank you,
Jo Ann

And just like that: plink! Another task landed on her ever-expanding to-do list. Wait, how did she get involved in this upgrade project? *We just enter the data and cut the checks,* she thought. She sighed as she scanned her calendar for an available time to propose to Jo Ann. With a hasty reply sent, she turned back to searching for her document.

"Hey, Avery, got a sec?" This time it was Sandy, her part-time administrative aide. "I think we have a bit of a problem."

"Problem?" Avery asked. The question pulled her out of a fog. "What's going on?"

"I was looking at the schedule, trying to help Dennis find a room for his training class?" Sandy was one of those people who pose every sentence as a question.

Avery remained quiet, waiting for Sandy to continue. She finally interjected, "And?"

"And, it looks like the IT lab is already booked for some sort of software evaluation, and the training rooms are also booked. Dennis doesn't know what he's supposed to do. Should he cancel the class?"

"Um, OK, let's take a look." Avery left with Sandy to view the calendar at the admin desk. They studied the availability and finally concluded Dennis could, in fact, move his class to the following week and still conduct his workshop. "Since it's for internal employees, I'm less concerned about rescheduling this one," Avery explained to Sandy. "If it were for citizens, it would be a problem, but we can just inform whoever signed up that we had to reschedule them."

"Oh, thank you, Avery!" Sandy said, "Dennis and I weren't sure what to do."

Avery left feeling oddly satisfied from the exchange. She hadn't produced much lately, so this small intervention made her feel useful. "I only wish I could be that productive all the time," she muttered.

NEW REALIZATIONS

It was one of those beautiful October days when the air is crisp and clean—short-sleeve weather that beckons you outdoors into the fresh air with the cool, fall breeze on your face. Those were the days Jon loved the most. You could work hard but not get overheated. Lunch in the sun was pleasant and not punishing. He daydreamed about those long-gone days as an employee when he just showed up to work, was given an assignment, and worked until he was done.

His days were different now, filled with countless meetings where Jon was required to evaluate options, compare information, and make an informed decision. People turned to him for his opinion, and then listened. Lord help you if you weren't paying attention and then made something up or tried to fake a decision. Jon was now swimming in a lane with people who held robust conversations and deliberated problems thoughtfully. Jon's decisions had real consequences to real people—his team—and impacted others in the department and the organization. For example, if Jon determined his crew could shore up a site in six hours, the department planned for and budgeted for that time frame. Overages, therefore, produced dramatic consequences to future budgets. Jon's decisions, in other words, didn't just impact one or two people, like making the wrong choice on where to go to lunch. Instead, his decisions impacted the trajectory of many other people: his crew, engineering staff, operations staff, administration, and citizens. The weight of the impact of his decisions often left him feeling small and incompetent.

He thought back to those times when he would simply show up to work, lunch pail in one hand, water bottle in the other, greeting his coworkers with a happy "hey, hey!" and dishing about the previous night's game. Things were simple then. If someone showed up cranky from a fight with his spouse the night before, Jon could be an easy hero by putting on his goofy act and cheering them up. The goofier he was, the more helpful he could be to his coworker. It was a good day if he could ease the pressures on his friends by making them laugh.

But as their supervisor, Jon was now bearing witness to heavy burdens, not little problems. He discovered some of his employees weren't just sad for a few hours or a day, but rather suffered from debilitating depression that required professional intervention; one of his employees suffered from traumatic grief due to losing a child; others battled health problems, like obesity, creating the more chronic conditions of heart disease or diabetes. Like him, some released life's stresses with a few beers after work, or a "little of the marijuana," as he would say. But for others, those recreational drugs weren't effective to dull the pain, so they turned to stronger things like opioids or cocaine.

Last Thursday morning, Jon held back one of his employees. His eyes were bloodshot, his hair and clothing soaked with the stench of stale cigarette smoke and alcohol from the night before. "You can't be here today," he said, firmly but with compassion, as he led him away from the crews. Why hadn't he realized how much his employee, Terry, was suffering? As his colleague, Jon would just tell Terry to not clock in, go home, and sleep it off. Now, as a supervisor, he was required to follow company procedures, which called for testing at the local clinic. It was all so much more complicated and important now. He was obligated to make sure everyone was safe on the job. *I can't have people working under the influence,* he reminded himself as he accompanied his employee to the clinic.

The particular meeting that was messing with his groove on such a gorgeous fall day was about personnel budgets and contingency plans for potential budget shortfalls. As the talk moved to possible reductions in personnel, Jon thought about Ivan, his newest crew member, whose youngest child required dialysis until a transplant could happen. Ivan needed this job, in a way that Jon never did. And what about his senior crew leads, Carlos and Emile, who devoted so much of their lives to the job? How could he ever consider sacrificing one of them when they gave so much? Was there ever an easy answer to workforce reductions? While he knew these were just talks, with little possibility for layoffs to occur, it made his stomach ache. He was beginning to understand the different layers of responsibility he carried as a supervisor. And, more often than not, he felt inadequate as a leader.

In one of their Moving into Leadership workshops, the facilitator emphasized, "When you step into a leadership position, you are now an agent of the organization. You represent the organization, and the decisions you make must be in the best interests of the organization."

Jon recalled challenging her on this point, as he did on so many others. "Oh no," he argued, "I'm here for my guys. My responsibility is to make sure they're taken care of."

"But our employees are here because of the organization," countered Keith, the IT manager. "My responsibility is to make sure my employees are doing what the organization needs."

"Yes, but if you don't have happy employees," Barbara added, "then you won't get good performance."

"True," Keith agreed. "But my primary purpose isn't to satisfy my employees. It's to satisfy the needs of my shareholders. I mean, we don't have shareholders here, because we don't make a profit here, but you know what I mean. We're here working for the citizens."

"Can we ever consider both?" Avery asked. "We need to consider the needs of the organization, but also advocate for the needs of our team, too."

As Jon recalled the rich debate, he realized it was one of the first times in his life that he felt unsure of his opinion because of a discussion. It wouldn't be the last time his deeply held values and beliefs would be challenged by new circumstances. He turned and looked, once again, out the conference room window, watching the clouds slip through the sky.

He glanced at an incoming text from Jimmy: "You approved my entire crew for a week off?" The text included numerous question marks.

Jon replied with a single one and wondered *What on earth is he talking about?*

Jimmy's response was lightning-fast. "You approved my entire crew—Jay, Dillon, and Sam—to be off next week."

Jon sighed, suddenly realizing the error he made. *Ugh. What have I gotten myself into?*

Leading a team is not about more work; it's about doing different work. What's your assessment of how Jon is managing his time and balancing his responsibilities as a leader? Why do you suppose things are falling through the cracks for Jon? What seems to be getting in his way?

Avery seems to be getting swallowed up by paperwork and tasks and is missing out on a crucial opportunity to connect and communicate with her staff. If she continues to cancel team meetings, what impact will that have on her team?

What are you noticing about the new responsibilities Jon's facing and how he's viewing his role?

chapter 5

A New Employee
Comes on Board

AVERY ESTIMATED THAT SHE SPENT a full day simply reviewing resumes for an open payroll position. Add to that several planning meetings with HR, followed by two days of back-to-back interviews, and it was easy to see how the entire process dominated her work schedule.

A lot of things had been put on hold during the recruitment process, including the new process maps and vendor research for that new performance management system. It was everything she could do to keep up with daily items while conducting this recruitment. She still had to be there for her employees, who seemed to need a lot of hand-holding and direction these past few weeks.

Despite it all, Avery was relieved to have found such a qualified candidate for her vacancy. Out of the two finalists, Avery selected Dave Wilson, a bright and soft-spoken college graduate with some recent payroll experience. Although Lisa in Human Resources preferred a different candidate, after some discussion she conceded that Dave's previous experience with payroll and his accounting degree gave him an edge. Plus, Avery appreciated his sense of humor and his easygoing personality.

She recounted the process to one of her colleagues, Christina, as they met in her office one afternoon.

"Yeah, that was quite the recruitment," Avery said. "HR really has us dotting our i's and crossing our t's. I was getting kinda frustrated there for a while, but I guess in the end it all worked out. I think the new guy's going to be great."

Several weeks flew by, as they always seemed to do, with a minor emergency here and there, and Avery found herself at the close of another week. She had just heard that her uncle had been hospitalized, and her mother wanted her to fly home for the weekend. As Avery hung up the call with her mother, a calendar reminder for Monday popped up: "Dave's first day."

Dave. The new guy. Starting this Monday. Avery sighed heavily.

"Ah, dang," she said out loud. "What am I going to do?"

Avery thought for a few minutes. It would be a hassle to extend his start date this late in the game, and she was committed to flying home to see her uncle. *What to do?*

I'll put Alice in charge of getting Dave started. She's been here forever and knows payroll inside and out.

Avery quickly headed over to Alice's cubicle, catching her as she was packing to leave for the weekend.

"Hey, Alice, I'm glad I caught you. I wanted to remind you that our new payroll analyst, Dave Wilson, starts on Monday. Unfortunately, I just found out my uncle is going into the hospital this weekend and I need to be in San Diego. Can you be Dave's first-day buddy? Show him around? Show him the ropes and get him acclimated?"

"I guess so," Alice's reply was dull. "Has he done HR's orientation?" she asked. "Yes," Avery confirmed. *Could she show a little more enthusiasm?* she thought, a little perturbed by Alice's lack of interest in what Avery thought was an important task.

"He should be ready on that front. We just need to get him trained on Wynsome and orient him to our payroll process. Remember? You liked Dave in the interview. He has some experience in payroll, so I think he'll be a quick study."

"Oh, is he the younger guy?" Alice asked. "Yeah, I wasn't sure who you finally chose."

"Thanks, I appreciate it." Avery said, taking her response as agreement for the task. "Please make sure he feels comfortable and give him the insider's overview of Wynsome. He can probably start by reviewing old payroll actions. I'll be back, hopefully by Wednesday, and will take it from there."

ROLLING OUT THE NON-WELCOME MAT

Dave Wilson was excited to begin his new job. While he had done a bit of accounting and payroll at Buddy's Fitness Center, he was mostly an assistant and didn't have a lot of opportunity to apply his accounting degree. His new boss, Avery Daniels, had explained during the interview process that his job would be payroll and helping with any special projects that came up in the department. He liked that she was willing to give him new opportunities to expand his skills. "If you're willing to learn," she told him, "I'm willing to train. And there's so much going on here, including software upgrades and a focus on process streamlining."

Axion offered loads of advancement opportunity, which was attractive to Dave, who had a family to support and a young daughter with special needs. Finally, he would have job security, good benefits, and a training ground to expand in the accounting field. It was a home run for him.

Dave had already completed Axion's Welcome Packet for new employees while at home. The Human Resources Department sent a series of webinars explaining Axion's antiharassment, diversity and inclusion, and antidiscrimination policies. An extensive packet of information on employee conduct, benefits, and leave was also emailed to him in advance of the plant's formal orientation, slated for two weeks after his first day. The email from HR informed him that his badge and parking pass would be waiting for him at the reception desk. "You may receive additional introductory instructions directly from your department," the notice said. Receiving none, Dave figured he was all set to go.

He left his house early Monday morning with plenty of time to arrive for his eight o'clock start time. As he pulled into the complex, he was delayed at the guard station. "I'm new. Just starting today," Dave explained. The guard station didn't have his name on the roster of new employees, but after a few minutes on the phone, waved him on through. Dave was confused that his name wasn't on the list but shrugged it off as a minor lapse (*Avery must've forgotten to give my name to security*) as he pulled into the parking area.

He noticed the employee parking lot required a permit, which he didn't yet have, so he chose a visitor's space, making a mental note to move his car later. *The instructions from HR said to pick up my parking pass and badge at the front desk,* he remembered.

Dave introduced himself to the receptionist, who was just arriving. "Nice to meet you," she said warmly. "Do you know where you're going? Top of the stairs, to the right," she directed. "Have a great day!" she called after him.

Dave headed up the short flight of stairs to the second floor. Lights in the building were beginning to flicker on. It was a little before eight in the morning, so few employees were in yet. Dave gave a tentative "hello?" into the hallway, hoping someone was there to greet him.

In seconds, he heard slight footsteps coming from the back hallway.

"Good morning ..." came a woman's voice. "Are you Dave?" she asked.

"I am!" Dave answered, spinning around to see Alice Franklin.

"I'm Alice. You may not remember me, but I was in your first round of interviews. Welcome!"

"Thanks," Dave replied.

"We're so glad to have you, Dave. I don't know if Avery told you?"

Dave looked puzzled and shook his head "no."

"She had to unexpectedly go home to San Diego. Someone in her family was having surgery this weekend, but she asked me to show you around and get you started."

Dave did his best to mask a tinge of disappointment that his new boss wasn't going to be there for his first day. He had an image of his boss greeting him with a warm welcome and a tour, and maybe the entire team greeting him on his first morning with donuts or something that said, "We're happy you're here."

You're such an idiot, he chastised himself.

Alice's cheery voice interrupted his thoughts, "Don't worry, it's pretty par for the course. You'll get used to all the dropped balls around here. I'm excited to show you around and get you started. Do you drink coffee?"

Because he gave a decided "yes," his tour began with the break room.

Alice continued her exposé on the department while they fixed themselves cups of coffee. Dave shifted his backpack that contained a few supplies and a picture of his wife and little girl from shoulder to shoulder.

"There are a few of us who prefer to get here extra early, when it's calm and quiet. And that way, I miss rush hour each way. I have a long commute, and I find I get so much done before everyone else gets here! You'll learn that there are some who show up whenever they dang-well please ..." her voice trailed off. Dave couldn't tell if she was joking or perturbed.

Next, Alice walked him through the building, introducing him to the other team members who were beginning to arrive. "We're a secret clan," she winked, returning him to the back area that housed Accounting and escorting him to his new office. "Take a few minutes to get settled, and I'll be back shortly to get you logged into our payroll system."

He began to put his few personal items in the desk drawer, noticing that the person who previously used the office was messy. There were old candy wrappers, twist ties, and crumpled tissues mixed in with assorted paper clips and Post-it notes. He rifled through some old file folders left behind, which contained things like outdated employee newsletters and policy statements on harassment and employee leave. He dumped them in the dented metal trash can next to his desk. He was setting out the picture on his desk when Alice returned and informed him that IT had not yet created his email account.

"Something about they didn't get advance notice?" she explained. "I talked to my buddy in IT, and they should have you set up by late morning."

"Cute," she said, nodding at the picture now displayed on his desk. "OK, well, let's get you a user account in our software system, which is called Wynsome. We refer to it as 'Wynsome lose some' because it's always crashing and does nothing that we need it to do." Her sarcasm hung in the room. She flicked on his PC and pulled over the extra chair in the corner, making herself comfortable next to him. "You'll find that most of the systems we work with here are pretty old. I'll teach you as many shortcuts as I can, but it's a pretty outdated system."

"I probably wouldn't be able to tell," Dave confessed.

Alice reached across him, clicking on the icon to launch Wynsome. "Mind?" she asked, motioning him to trade places with her. Now seated in front of his PC, she expertly logged in, and in a few clicks, created his user login.

"You'll need to go in and change your password to one you want," she instructed. "What system have you worked with at your last job?"

"I don't remember what it was called," he replied. "I think they actually created it in-house or one of the owner's friends designed it. It was pretty simple. Not a lot of bells and whistles."

"Let me show you a few basic functions; then I'll turn you loose to explore on your own," she said. Dave watched as Alice demonstrated some of the basic functions of Wynsome and a few shortcuts, such as how to search for employees.

"Pretty easy?" she asked.

He shrugged. "Seems pretty straightforward," he said. "It might take me a bit, but I think I can handle it."

"Good," she said. "Tell you what," she continued, getting up from his chair, "I'll bring you some old payroll entry forms, and you can dink around in the system—see what you can make sense of."

She returned in a few minutes, with two thick manila file folders and a fresh cup of coffee for herself.

"First, study these personnel action forms and familiarize yourself with our pay rates. Then, I want you to log into Wynsome and try to locate these old payroll action forms. Don't worry; you can't mess anything up because they're approved actions. But look around and get familiar with the different reports we use, and practice what you already learned. I'll check back with you, and we can sit down and enter some actual forms together when I return. Sound good?" She closed down the software, forcing him to log back in, then left him to work on his own. "Sorry about the delay with your email and stuff," she offered, as she stood in his doorway. "You'll find that's pretty typical for how things are done around here. Did you get your badge and your parking pass?"

"No, not yet," he said.

"If you go back down to the front desk, Missy will make your badge and your parking pass."

After he returned, badge affixed on a lanyard around his neck and parking pass in hand, he settled in to review the information in the two dense folders Alice left behind. A few employees stopped by to introduce themselves. He was grateful for the outreach.

It felt like an exceptionally long time until Alice returned to check on his progress. "Good work, Dave. You're a fast learner," she said. "So now I have some actual personnel action forms that need simple things entered, such as address changes. Try your hand, then let me know when you're finished, and we'll review together. OK?"

"Sounds good," he told her. He worked diligently on the project she gave him, but before long, his stomach was growling loudly. With no sign from Alice, at around twelve thirty, he peeked his head into her office to inquire about lunch.

"Is there anything I need to know about lunches here? Do we go whenever, or is there a set time? What does the team usually do?"

"Sorry about that," she said. "I keep forgetting all this is new for you." She explained that Avery is easygoing about breaks and lunches.

"As long as the work is getting done, Avery doesn't care when you take your lunch or breaks. Just don't abuse the privilege."

"Do you all go to lunch together?" he asked.

"Sometimes, but usually we all just do our own thing. We're not an exceptionally tight group here. I tend to bring my lunch, but some of the others head off campus for lunch," she told him.

Dave opted to leave for lunch, and when he returned, his entrance went smoothly now that he possessed his official badge. He rolled down his window at the guard gate. "Just want to formally introduce myself this time," he said to the guard on duty. "Dave Wilson, Payroll."

Back in his office, he finished the last of the payroll change forms and walked over to Alice's office to request more.

She was eating her sandwich at her desk. "Just wanted to let you know I finished those entries," he announced.

"Those didn't take you long at all!" she said. "We should probably go over them together, but let me see what else I can scrounge up for you to work on."

Dave couldn't tell if the day moved quickly or at a snail's pace. He was a little discouraged by what didn't happen. His boss wasn't there; he didn't have an email account; and the work, while new to him, felt almost too simple. He wanted to be able to jump in and learn more, but he felt like Alice was limited in what she could give him. He wasn't sure if he would be happy with what felt like busywork to him. Is this what the job is? If so, it's different from how it was described to him in the interview. As he headed to his car at the end of the day, the thought crossed his mind that perhaps this wasn't a good fit for him. *Maybe I should cut my losses,* he thought. He decided to talk with his spouse about whether he was going to return the next day.

TOO LITTLE, TOO LATE

Avery returned to work Wednesday morning, irritable from so much time spent with her family at the hospital. She dropped off her bag in her office, turned on her PC, then headed down the hallway to grab some coffee.

She passed by Dave's cubicle, and finding it empty, continued to her early bird's office. "Good morning, Alice," she said. "How are you?"

"Good," Alice replied. "How's your dad doing?"

"Uncle. He's fine. Everything went just fine. How're things here? How's Dave doing?" she asked, motioning down the hall toward his office.

"I think OK," Alice replied. "Is he not here yet? He's been early both days."

"No, he doesn't appear to be. When you see him, would you ask him to stop by so we can connect? I have my weekly meeting with Ken, but that should take only an hour."

"Of course," Alice said, and Avery moved on to her next obligation with Ken, followed by the monthly senior managers' meeting.

The morning slipped past her, and Avery realized she hadn't yet seen Dave. She was just about to pick up the phone to call over to his office when he showed up at her office, rapping softly.

"Good morning," he said. "I was told you wanted to see me?"

"Dave!" she said, motioning him into her office. "So glad to finally get to connect with you. I'm so sorry I couldn't be here for your first few days. Are you getting settled in OK?" she asked.

"You bet," he replied.

"Well, we have a lot to go over," Avery began. "First, I want to hear everything about what you and Alice have been doing. Then, I think I want to set you up to shadow Lindsay. Payroll runs next Tuesday morning, and I want you shadowing her, up and until we do that run."

They chatted for several minutes, but Dave was a bit hesitant to ask questions of Avery. He hadn't spent much time with her yet, and she seemed like a distant authority figure, rather than an accessible boss. He hoped this would change as they spent more time together. He still had a lot of unanswered questions for Avery, such as:

- What are the primary responsibilities of this job?
- How will I be evaluated?
- How should I prioritize my work?
- Who do I report to with questions or concerns? Is it Avery? Alice? Lindsay?

Dave headed over to the break room and fixed an iced coffee for himself, then emailed Lindsay, requesting time with her. The rest of the day he surfed the internet while he waited to hear back from Lindsay. He felt guilty being so idle, but he didn't know how else to occupy his time. The day crept along until finally, at quitting time, Dave was the first to leave.

Take a moment to reflect on your most recent "first day on the job." Was it a positive experience, a so-so one, or a negative one? To what can you attribute that rating?

Onboarding is a core responsibility of leaders, but it's more than "orienting" your employees to policies and procedures. It sets the stage for a successful future. What should/could Avery have done differently to effectively orient Dave to the organization, the team, and his job? (Notice all the "little things" that weren't in place for him: no notice at the front gate; dirty office; no badge; no parking pass; and, of course, no boss!)

What components do you believe should be part of every employee's first day, first week, and first few months on the job? You may want to take some time and create a list for yourself of everything new employees would want and need to know on their first day/week/month of a new job. Use this initial list as the foundation for your own onboarding program.

How do you think a more structured, thoughtful, and positive onboarding experience would make a difference in Dave's tenure at Axion?

chapter 6

CORE RESPONSIBILITIES AND DECIDING TO DELEGATE

THE MOVING INTO LEADERSHIP SESSION began with an interesting discussion about leadership. "In our workplaces today," the facilitator began, "we often substitute the term leadership when speaking about supervision or management. Most of you have been given the title of supervisor or manager. That carries with it certain responsibilities and expectations. Your role is to ensure that certain outcomes occur on your team.

"Leadership, on the other hand," she continued, "is often understood more broadly. There is a lot of debate about this. Some scholars point out that leadership is different from the technical act of supervision or management. Leadership, they argue, is not limited to a title and refers to a wide range of behaviors necessary to build trust and influence."

"I don't know about you," Doug said, "but I know plenty of supervisors who are not leaders."

"That is sometimes the case, yes," replied the facilitator. "Sometimes people are promoted to supervisor and think that they simply have to demonstrate their superior technical knowledge. But supervising a team requires *leadership*. What I want for you all," she said, pausing to survey the room, "is the confidence to manage the technical aspects of your roles while leading, influencing, and inspiring your teams."

The class reviewed the traditional distinction between management, "which is typically understood as maintaining correct operations, procedures, and production," and leadership, which the facilitator described as "building future capability."

"In so many organizations today," the facilitator continued, "the responsibilities of supervising, managing, and leading a team are often rolled together. There will be times when you must make sure the correct things get done.

"What are some examples of the things we do that ensure the work of the organization is accomplished?" the facilitator asked. She divided the large whiteboard in half, titling one side "Management Responsibilities." The group members were slow to offer their ideas, but with a bit of coaxing, they began to identify various tasks and outcomes associated with "getting work done through others." The facilitator scribbled quickly on the whiteboard as they offered examples such as budget reports, payroll, pipes laid ("Your role is to ensure pipes are laid correctly," the facilitator clarified), samples tested ("Again, making sure sampling is done per standard," she corrected), and so forth until the class created a list of management responsibilities.

"There are also times when you must build potential on your team. This is the relationship side. The way in which we accomplish output in an organization is important. *How* do we get a team of diverse people to work together, cooperate, and communicate so they produce results? This is the leadership imperative," she explained.

The group brainstormed once again, this time identifying the strategies and techniques needed to build relationships and create a dynamic team. On the other side of the board, the facilitator posted their ideas about building relationships and leading others:

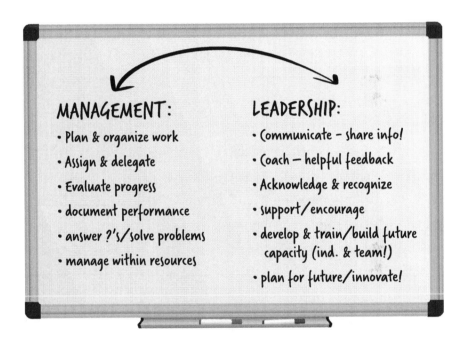

MANAGEMENT:
- Plan & organize work
- Assign & delegate
- Evaluate progress
- document performance
- answer ?'s/solve problems
- manage within resources

LEADERSHIP:
- Communicate – share info!
- Coach – helpful feedback
- Acknowledge & recognize
- support/encourage
- develop & train/build future capacity (ind. & team!)
- plan for future/innovate!

"The challenge we have in organizations today is to balance the need to produce outcomes with the need to motivate and create talent. Tasks *and* relationships matter," the facilitator explained, as she drew arrows between both columns on the whiteboard, illustrating the interdependency of both.

"I don't know about anyone else," Barbara, a supervisor from the lab began, "but this seems like an awful lot to do and keep up with my own work. I mean, how am I supposed to do all this *and* handle my responsibilities, too?"

Her comment created waves of agreement and side conversations across the room.

"It's such a great question, Barbara, and a common misconception. You see, your job *is* all these things. When leading a team, our role is to support our team members while they do the work."

The facilitator sensed a current of disapproval, so she continued, "When you step into a leadership position, it's no longer about you. As an individual performer, your job is to make yourself look good and to demonstrate your skill and expertise to others. But when leading a team, your focus must shift to helping others become more proficient—hopefully, more proficient than you are. And when your team performs well, it's a positive reflection of your leadership ability."

"And when they don't?" asked Keith.

"That, too, is a reflection of us," she said. "Over the course of this program, we'll be learning techniques, tools, and skills to strengthen our ability to not only manage performance but build internal talent and capacity—to lead others. It will be a balance of both, because both are vital in our organizations today."

Sensing the need, the facilitator released the class for its morning break. Jon filed out of the room and headed for the coffee. On the break, he complained to another participant while they helped themselves to coffee.

"My thing is," Jon began, "this isn't realistic. Leadership in my line of work is very different from leadership in, say, engineering or accounting." He was dissatisfied with the program and its content because he was looking for tangible methods to get his guys to hustle. His crew, he felt, were far too apathetic, and Jon felt as though he had to constantly push and prod them to get even the simplest tasks accomplished.

While Avery wasn't involved in the conversation, she overheard and stepped forward. "I don't know," Avery interjected, "I think leadership is probably similar regardless of your line of work."

"You don't know my guys," Jon replied.

WORKING AROUND THE CLOCK

"How many of you are coming to work early to get caught up?" Several people in the class raised their hands.

"And are any of you staying late, after everyone else has gone, to get caught up?"

Several more participants admitted to this. "Some of you, I see," the facilitator pointed out, "are both coming in early and staying late."

Jon was one of those participants. "It's probably going to be like this for a while," he admitted to his wife one evening after she began to complain about his late schedule. "At least until I get these crews going."

"I'm beginning to think there's another woman!" she teased him.

"While there may be legitimate reasons to occasionally come in early or stay late," the facilitator explained, "end-of-year bonuses on a payroll run, for example," with a nod to Avery, "in most cases, if you find yourself burning the candle at both ends, it may be that you've not yet perfected the art of delegation, and that's the subject of our session today.

"As we've already discussed numerous times, one of the hardest things about stepping into a leadership position is transitioning from doing the work to supporting others as they perform. From the beginning of our program, I've emphasized the importance of trusting your employees to do their jobs. It's so hard for us as leaders, especially those of us who have spent years perfecting our craft, to step aside and let others do the work instead!"

"I don't want my team to think I'm dumping stuff on them," Phyllis, an Operations supervisor, shared.

"I struggle with that as well," Brad chimed in. "I mean, my staff members have enough on their plates, and I hesitate to add any more responsibility."

Jon finally couldn't hold back any longer and spoke up. "My team knows I have their backs, but I have to be really careful about what I give them. They need my direction; otherwise, they can easily get overwhelmed and that can lead to mistakes. But they know they can count on me to help them out of a jam or to make their jobs easier."

"And," Jon continued, feeling the need to further explain, "they know I care about them and wouldn't bury them. If I can help them out, I will."

"I can tell, Jon, that you care very much for all your team members. How do you suppose your care and consideration for them, and your willingness to help them out, impacts your team?" the facilitator asked.

There was silence in the room. The facilitator rephrased the question. "Does Jon's desire to be kind, helpful, and giving to his team members help them? Or hinder them?"

Someone else immediately responded, "It helps them, of course." It seemed a silly question.

"OK, so helping out a team member in a jam may be helpful in the moment. You get a task done or help out your team. But what about over the long term? If you're constantly stepping in to help your team members, lend them a hand, or show them how to do something, how do you think that might impact them?"

The facilitator paused, waiting for an answer from the group, but seeing confusion, reiterated her question. "Think about it in a slightly different way," she continued. "How many of you consider yourselves experts?" Some hands went up, including Jon's. Others were a little hesitant.

"I think I'm an expert in some aspects of my job," Avery clarified.

"Makes sense," the facilitator responded. She asked the full group, "If you have the opportunity to demonstrate your expertise, are you likely to do so?"

"I think I'm supposed to do that!" Jon replied, again with exasperation in his voice.

"Sometimes," the facilitator replied. "Sometimes there will be situations where you need to teach or keep someone from harm. There are times when our role is to instruct or guide. But, in general, the role of a leader is to build expertise in others, not to demonstrate our own abilities.

"Delegation," she continued, "is the art of handing a task, a responsibility, or a decision to someone else so they develop, learn, and grow. But here's the problem: When we give tasks to others—especially tasks that we're experts in—we no longer have control over how that task is accomplished, when it's completed, and whether it's completed exactly the way we would do it. Have you ever been in that situation where you've watched someone else botch a task that you could do with your eyes closed?"

Groans came from the room. "Too many times," came one response.

"That's often why supervisors or managers don't give the work away," she said. "It's that old adage, 'If you want something done right ...'" her voice trailed off as the rest of the room filled in the rest with a hearty "... do it yourself!"

"What are some other reasons why we're not likely to delegate?" The facilitator helped the group come up with a list of reasons, including:

- It's easier to do it yourself.
- It's quicker to do it yourself.
- You enjoy doing the task.
- You're the only one who knows how to do it.
- You don't trust your employees to do the task properly.
- You don't want to overload your employees with any more work.
- You don't want to upset your employees by giving them more work, or tasks that might challenge or frustrate them.

"Let's say, Jon, you meet up with one of your crews and you see them struggling to replace a section of pipe. What are your options for how to help them?" the facilitator asked.

"Well, I take a look at the problem, and I can probably show them how to do it, pretty quickly, or sometimes I let them help me," he explained. "Actually, I know I can replace a stick of pipe a lot quicker than any of 'em!" he boasted to the person sitting next to him.

"And when you stepped in and fixed the problem, how did that impact your day?"

Jon was quick to reply, "It made me feel good that I can help."

"And when they encounter the same problem, perhaps the next day, what is your response to the team? Will you go back out there and demonstrate again?"

Jon began to stir a bit in his seat. "Well, I would hope they would've watched and learned when I did it the first time! I'll probably be annoyed to have to show them again," he admitted.

"I think I'm beginning to see where you're going with this," Avery piped in. "Are you saying that by doing the work for them, Jon is making them dependent on him?"

"That's part of it, yes," the facilitator explained. "Can we all for a moment imagine a different response that Jon could have used when he showed up at that job site and found his team struggling?"

Another participant, Elliott, took a stab. "We're all under pretty tight deadlines here at the plant and need to be doing things as quickly and efficiently as possible," he argued.

"And is it efficient for Jon, at his salary, to be running an excavator? Or repairing a leak? Is that his role for the organization?" the facilitator countered. "What happens when Jon has several crews out on job sites, each of which have line breaks, equipment failures, or problems they can't diagnose or solve on their own?"

The facilitator paused to let this scenario sink in with the class. She then continued, "In fact, if Crew B doesn't know how to solve its problem without Jon, what is that crew doing while Jon is helping Crew A?"

There were many side conversations happening around the room in response to the direction the discussion was going. The facilitator brought the room back to order and said, "Are Jon's crews more productive or less productive now that Jon is fixing their problems?"

"They're less productive," Avery announced. "Crew B, Crew C, Crew D—they can't do anything unless and until Jon gets there!"

"Precisely," the facilitator concluded. "Now, first of all, Jon, thank you for being such a good sport and letting me use you as an example so we can understand this concept. The point applies to all of us. And what we're talking about here is the possibility that we're actually doing our employees a disservice by solving their problems for them."

She turned to the class and asked, "How many of you are competent to solve complex problems in your department?" Hands furtively went up around the room. The group wasn't sure how or if to respond.

"Do you feel confident to solve problems, answer questions, and instruct your employees on how to do things properly or correctly?"

Participants were nodding and responding, "Well, yes, that's my job," and "You bet!"

"And how many of you feel as though it's your duty, your obligation, to demonstrate to your employees and to others that you are competent?"

The room fell silent, but Jon quickly spoke up. "I'm the boss because I know more than everyone else. That's why I was hired!" Many in the room nodded their agreement at his response.

She continued. "OK, and how many of your staff members have your level of competence?" There was silence in the room. "Let's think about it. What did we decide is the role of a supervisor, manager, or leader?"

This time Avery was the first to respond. "It's to be a resource so employees can perform successfully."

"I think we discussed that our role is to set goals and expectations, make sure people have the resources, and then support them in performing their jobs," Doug said.

"What is the impact on our employees, or on the team, if we have the attitude that we know more than they do or that we're better at things than they are?" the facilitator asked.

Keith spoke up next. "In my line of work, I can't possibly know all there is to know about our field. It's changing so rapidly I have to hope that my employees are staying current and are experts in their area."

"In fact," the facilitator continued, "if we're stepping in to do work that our employees could figure out on their own," she paused, "or *should* figure out on their own, I don't think we're helping. It takes us away from the high-level planning, organizing, observing, and feedback work we're supposed to be doing.

"If you're doing the work," the facilitator continued, "it doesn't help your employees gain new skills or knowledge they need to be independent performers."

"I'm ashamed to admit it," Avery interrupted, "but I had this happen not too long ago. I had an employee come to me with a problem—a pretty simple problem—and I just said, 'Let me handle it.'" Avery was remembering her brief encounter with Dennis regarding the catering charges for the employee party. "I took over for him, and I don't really think he wanted or needed me to! And I was so mad that I had another thing on my plate to do! But now I realize I actually gave more work to myself!"

"So, you mean you want us to let our employees struggle and figure things out, even if they don't know what they're doing? That doesn't sound productive. And it could be dangerous!" Elliott was showing signs of frustration.

"Not exactly, Elliott," the facilitator said. "We never want to put our employees at risk or in danger's way. But this is an excellent question. Let me ask the rest of the room. Go back to Jon's example. What could he have done differently with that crew at the job site?"

The room erupted with suggestions, including, "He could have asked the crew members for their ideas on how to solve the problem."

"That's an excellent approach," the facilitator said. "Why am I suggesting this is an excellent approach?"

"Well," Brad hesitated at first, then offered his idea. "I think if Jon asked the crew members how they wanted to proceed, he would learn how much they know. You know, if they're showing they know what to do, they can replace the pipe while Jon watches."

"Precisely," affirmed the facilitator. "But if their ideas were bad ones, or ideas that could be potentially dangerous or against protocol. Then what?"

"Well, if it was me, and my staff came up with something that would cost us more time …" Keith began.

"… or is a safety violation," Michelle interrupted.

"I'd want to steer them in a different direction," Keith said, finishing his thought.

"You bet, Keith," the facilitator said, "but the way we do this is important. If our employees are learning, and they're offering up ideas and trying to be proactive, we don't want to hinder that energy! We want to encourage that. The way we guide employees in their learning can result in a negative or a positive experience. Let me explain what I mean." She paused, giving the group a moment to digest the discussion so far.

"For example, if an employee gives me an answer that would be unsafe, or incorrect, I can say, 'No, we don't want to do that,' or 'No, we don't do it that way.' But will that motivate an employee to continue to come up with new ideas?

"On the other hand, I can ask her questions and get her to think through her ideas so she figures out on her own that it's not viable or why it's not viable. That's far more educational for her."

"Couldn't Jon just show them how to do it? Then they'll know for next time," another participant asked.

"Could he offer suggestions for them to try?" asked Avery.

"Yes, in fact, all of these are better options to help your employees figure things out on their own. Jon can be on the sidelines, making sure no one is risking his safety, or going too far off course, but it's a far better use of his time to coach his employees rather than do the work himself. Jon's focus should always be on building up the skills and knowledge of his crew members. After all, he can't be everywhere all the time!"

"Or can you, Jon?" the facilitator teased, with a wink his way.

Jon thought he was doing his team a great service by tackling the difficult tasks and giving them the easy ones. He thought they appreciated the fact that he jumped in the trenches and showed them how to do things. And he definitely thought it was his job to make things as easy as possible for his employees. He was dealing with low morale and was trying to get them to like their jobs! He had a hard time believing he was doing them a disservice or causing harm.

The facilitator interrupted his thoughts. "I want to make another very important point," she said. "How do you suppose Jon's employees might feel when Jon steps in and handles tasks for them? Or doesn't allow them to weigh in on how to solve a problem?"

The facilitator explained that while Jon's intentions are noble, he is unintentionally sending the message that he doubts his crew's competence.

Avery brought the conversation back to her own situation. "So, while I'm trying to be helpful, my employees may think I don't trust them?"

"Over time, that may be the message your actions send, yes."

The room started to buzz with side conversations, and the facilitator allowed this to take place for a few minutes before calling the group back to order. "Please remember, your job isn't to do their work. Your work is to support your team members and help them build their own skills. You know your stuff and are on the way to building new expertise. Let your employees develop their abilities. That's what they need from you."

The facilitator pressed the point to ensure the class was receiving the message. Leading a team is not an opportunity to don a cape and mask and prove you have superhero powers. Instead, "our purpose is to help *others* become superheroes." The facilitator drew out the point even more. "It's not about you."

This conversation finally piqued Jon's interest. He rolled things around in his head. Yes, it was true that he didn't really trust his crew, but that was because they made mistakes. They weren't as quick as he was. They weren't as efficient, and they certainly weren't as knowledgeable.

They're just not ready to take on more responsibility, he felt, *but once they spend more time with me, learning from me, then I can give them more complex tasks.*

But what if by restricting their involvement he was inadvertently sending the message he didn't believe they could do it? Did his crew sense this? Rather than take initiative, they waited to be told what to do. Or did they hold back because they knew he would step up and do the work himself? What a vicious, self-fulfilling prophecy this created: Once his team members stopped taking initiative, Jon felt justified to restrict them even more, then the crew felt devalued and did even less, which justified Jon's belief that they were unmotivated and lazy.

"I have to do everything around here," he complained to Stu one afternoon. "These guys, they don't do anything unless I tell them to. They'd just sit around and be lazy if it weren't for me." It was true, but Jon didn't inherit a team of passive workers. He created one by limiting their decision-making authority and strictly overseeing their work.

Jon was surprised by the realization that he could be the source of his crew's inaction. He hadn't given his crew the respect and freedom they needed to do their jobs. What else did he get backwards?

"When you lead others, you're not the important one. The team is," the facilitator concluded. "When we return from lunch, we'll learn some basic tips for delegation and help you begin to implement these strategies."

WHOSE JOB IS IT?

After lunch, and with his curiosity finally ignited, Jon put his phone in his pocket, and finally turned his attention to the facilitator.

"Now might be a good time for you to take a look at the work that's on your desk, or review the emails in your inbox, and ask yourself: Does all this work really belong to me, or can it be accomplished by someone else on my team?"

"Many experts[2] suggest keeping a journal of where you're spending your time. Ask yourself:

- Does someone already know how to do this task? If so, then give the task to that person.
- Could someone benefit by learning this task? Or, should someone else know how to do this task? If so, that person's also a good candidate for delegation.[3]

"Often, simply by habit, leaders perform routine tasks that could easily be reassigned to team members, and these team members might actually do a better job or learn from the task.

"Ask yourself," the facilitator continued, "do I really need to edit that article, or is someone else on the team a good writer? Who else can review this spreadsheet? Who would benefit from conducting a preliminary client intake meeting? Use any and every opportunity to delegate to your team members. Not only will this free up time for you to take on your own projects, but it will show your team members that:

- You trust them enough to give them more complex tasks.
- You believe in them and want to see them gain new skills.
- You value the unique abilities they bring to the team."

"How do I know which employees to delegate to?" Barbara asked.

"Talk to them," the facilitator replied. "Make sure you're not giving people tasks that are too complex. It may sound obvious, but you don't want to give work that's too complex to someone who is just learning. But if you're meeting with your employees and discussing how projects and tasks are going, you'll come to understand what people are capable of and what they're not. Just make sure they have the time, the tools, and the authority they need to accomplish the task.

"One of my mentors explained it this way," the facilitator said. "She said, 'I hope my team misses me when I'm away but doesn't need me.' Isn't that great? It means, if your unit functions brilliantly while you're away, it's a sign that you're doing an amazing job of creating a competent team that serves the organization well. You've developed a power team."

As the group concluded its session for the day, Jon's thoughts turned to one of his first jobs, as a mechanic, and his boss who boasted that he never took a vacation. He racked up so much vacation time that the HR Department finally forced him to take some time off. His excuses were "there's too much going on," and "this place would fall apart if I took a vacation." But the truth was this boss was using his position to feel important. He thought he brought so much to the team that they couldn't function without him. It made the team feel bad. *He never even gave us the chance to prove we could handle things on our own,* Jon recalled.

That mechanic, Jon realized, probably thought he was helping, but instead he did the entire organization a disservice. No workers gained new skills or advanced in their positions. *He never made any of us feel important, or smart,* Jon realized. Instead, that mechanic only gave Jon menial jobs, the lowest-level jobs, which made him feel incompetent. *None of us could think for ourselves or do our jobs without him hovering over us.* As Jon reflected on that early job, he remembered how frustrated and demoralized he felt, which was the reason he quit.

I'd forgotten about that time, Jon thought. *Wow, I don't want Carlos or Emile to feel like I don't trust them.*

As the class began to leave, the facilitator called out to them, "At our next session, I want to hear all about your attempts to delegate more." Instead of quickly gathering their notebooks to leave, this time the class members lingered behind, swapping stories, and comparing notes with each other.

for your consideration

The terms supervisor, manager, and leader are sometimes used interchangeably, but technically, anyone can lead—and in many, many cases leadership is happening in our organizations and our communities by people without formal positions of authority. In other words, it's commonly appreciated that you don't need a title (supervisor, manager, director, boss) to be a leader. What's your impression of the distinction between leadership and management? Have you led without the formal title or position? If so, what was your experience?

What part of your new role will be most challenging for you: managing the technical aspects of the job, such as reporting, or the interpersonal side of your role, such as coaching, training, delegating, and giving feedback? What training and education would be helpful for you to address these challenge areas?

By now you should have a greater understanding of the art of delegation. Why is delegation so important as a leader? How would you summarize some of the lessons Jon and Avery are learning about delegation?

chapter 7

LEARNING TO LEAD

JON HAD TO ADMIT, the last Moving into Leadership session made him uneasy. He thought long and hard about the message from that session. While it wasn't his intention, he had to wonder if he was the source of some of the problems plaguing his team.

It was true that he questioned the abilities of some of his crew members. But was that such a bad thing? There were others whom he did trust: Joey showed better judgment lately, Carlos was very knowledgeable, and Jimmy and Emile knew about as much as Jon. (About *as much,* he thought).

Still, this was his show, and if he gave the crews more responsibility and mistakes were made, it would be Jon's fault. Or worse yet, if someone got hurt, he could never forgive himself. *It's my butt on the line if they muck things up, not theirs!* he told himself. As a rule, he felt it better to be safe, rather than sorry.

With the memory of that old head mechanic still in his mind, perhaps some sort of compromise was in order. In what way, or what area, could he give the teams more? He thought long and hard about it and decided he could temporarily let crew leads handle scheduling employees. Maybe he could let crew leads organize their work schedules, too. *As long as they keep me in the loop.*

In the last Moving into Leadership session, the facilitator suggested that Jon wasn't allowing his employees the freedom to make their own decisions and perform their work independently.

"You mean, I'm the reason they're lazy?" he remembers challenging her.

"Actually, I would argue that you're the reason they're not confident, competent, and independent," the facilitator clarified.

"You see, the more you do for them, the more you send the message that you don't find them competent. It's unlikely they'll do more if you're sending the message you don't trust them."

"Huh?" Jon asked, perplexed by that convoluted statement.

The facilitator laughed. "What I mean is, it's a circle: If you don't trust your crew, you don't give them a lot to do, which tells them you don't want them to do a lot, so they only do the minimum. You interpret this as a lack of motivation, so then you give them even less to do, which they then interpret as 'he doesn't trust our ability,' so they do even less."

She paused. "It's a self-fulfilling prophecy."

"She means they know you don't trust them, so they just wait until you tell them what to do." This time Keith accurately interpreted for Jon.

"Oh," said Eva. "So, whatever I think they can't do, they can't."

"Yes," the facilitator replied.

"Remember, our role isn't to *do* the work, but to support our staff members who are doing the work. They may not always do things the way you would, but it's more important that they achieve the outcome you need."

Jon found the hardest part about all of this was the realization he's not in full control of what others are doing. "Unless there's a clear procedure or process," the facilitator explained, "once we turn over a task to someone else, we lose control over how it's done. And very often people will perform tasks differently than we would."

When Jon thought about it, he realized he doled out work to his crews. He gave them specific tasks to complete, but rarely described the project scope or purpose. He didn't explain what he needed by day's or week's end.

"Make sure your employees know time frames or deadlines," the facilitator explained, "and the qualities or standards they must achieve."

The class spent time discussing the point about quality and standards. Eddie, the benefits supervisor from HR, said, "I remember getting really frustrated with my team when it wasn't meeting my expectations. Turns out, my team members thought they were doing a great job, according to their standards! So we had to have a conversation about the quality I expected versus what they deemed to be quality work."

"This is an important point, Eddie," the facilitator replied. "If our employees are not meeting our expectations, we have to first ask ourselves, 'Have I clearly explained the time frames, costs, qualities, or standards?'"

Jon was tumbling the ideas over in his head. *How can I be sure my crew makes the right decisions?* he wondered. The facilitator explained that as long as employees know how to do the work, they should be free to work independently.

"What happens if they muck things up or make a mistake?" he asked.

The facilitator asked him to play that out. "What *would* happen if a mistake was made?"

"Well, for one thing, my crews deal with dangerous situations and heavy equipment, so people can get hurt if they make mistakes."

"That's an important concern, Jon," the facilitator said. "And in circumstances where safety is our highest priority, what is our role as leaders?"

Barbara, from the lab, chimed in this time. "I think we have to ensure that our employees know safety guidelines and have been taught what our safety protocols are. But we can't do the work for them."

"My job is to make sure everyone knows how to be safe on the job," Doug, a supervisor in Operations, added.

"I always want people to work safely," the facilitator stated, pausing to make sure the point was received. "No one wants to have a regulatory or safety violation at the utility. Mistakes may happen, but our role is to make sure our employees have the equipment they need to work safely, and they are regularly trained on how to work safely."

Jon replied, almost under his breath, "I could never forgive myself if anything happened to anyone on my crews."

"I know, Jon," the facilitator acknowledged. "None of us ever wants harm to come to someone else. I think Barbara makes an excellent point that it may be our responsibility to train our employees to work safely, because you can't be everywhere. So let's talk about what we can do as leaders to build that ability in our employees.

"If you focused your attention on making sure they were fully prepared to work safely, would that give you more confidence to send them out to work on their own?"

Jon looked a bit perplexed as he thought through the distinction.

"Rather than doing the work for them, if you felt confident in *how* they worked, would you feel more comfortable sending them out to work independently?"

Jon nodded that he would, as did others in the room.

"It seems to me," the facilitator said, seeking to conclude the discussion, "that once employees know what they are supposed to do (the expectation) and how they're supposed to do it (following these safety protocols)—once we put our energy into giving our employees those guidelines—then we ought to be able to trust them enough to do their jobs."

"This applies a bit differently to us in IT," said Keith, "because, while my team members aren't necessarily working with dangerous equipment, I want them to be able to coach each other and help each other avoid rabbit holes and diversions that aren't necessarily productive."

"An excellent point," the facilitator replied, "because as Patrick Lencioni[4] tells us, the height of teamwork is when team members hold each other accountable. It's powerful when employees are helping each other work effectively or safely."

A LITTLE LETTING GO

Despite his reticence, Jon decided to give his team more responsibility and more independence. He wasn't quite sure how it was all going to play out, how he was going to do it, or how he was going to feel about it, but he was committed to giving it a try. He didn't understand how not working closely with each crew was more effective or more productive, but he cared about his teams and he wanted to be successful as their boss. So if that meant he had to do things a bit differently, then he owed it to himself to try.

The next morning, he announced his new intentions at his morning meeting. "You guys, I'm starting to get really busy," he said, which was only partly a fib, "with some new capital projects coming up, so I'm going to need you all to help pick up some of the slack. From now on, I won't be able to be on job sites as much as I have been. It's gonna be up to you all to work together to solve problems as they arise."

The crew members looked furtively around at each other. There were whispers and side conversations that occurred. "Hold on, hold on now," Jon said. "Here's the deal. You all know your jobs. And you're gonna have to step things up. As we head into a new season, you know we're going to start to have a lot more main breaks and leaks happening. So be prepared. And we have a lot of scheduled maintenance to take care of, too, which you all are capable of handling. So, I need everybody to step it up."

The room was so abuzz that the crews barely heard Jon announce "Instead of me, crew leads will schedule daily assignments. And they'll submit end-of-week reports to me." Then he added, loudly enough to be heard over the din, "You will still likely see me throughout the week." The group quieted down with that announcement. "But I won't be taking as much of a hands-on approach as I have been."

With that, Jon handed over the schedule of maintenance projects for pipe replacements at several locations and pulled Emile aside. "Emile, you guys head out to Howard and Fifth. Reports of low pressure at the main line. Check it out, and let me know what you all think is necessary."

"You got it," Emile said, hustling to grab his gear as he left. Jon knew Emile was competent to assess the situation, but he still wanted to be on site himself. *Baby steps,* he thought. It was going to be very challenging for him to let go. He watched as his crews headed out for the day.

Jon shared his new strategy with Stu a few days later. "It's so weird, Stu," he said. The two of them were the first to arrive for a scheduled conference call, and they were catching up on Jon's "great experiment," as he had come to call it.

"What's so weird?" Stu asked him.

"Well, to be honest, it feels like I'm not needed!" Jon replied. He was joking a little, but then again, he wasn't. He was feeling a little like the unpopular kid not invited to the party. "Everyone seems to be doing just fine without me," he confessed.

"I think the important thing is you're available if they need you," Stu explained. "They're all competent. After all, you pretty much trained them all."

"True," Jon said. "Very true." He was beginning to see that there still might be a role for him to play.

Over the next few weeks, Jon's crews stepped up to the challenge. The teams were timely each morning and hustled throughout the day. Crew leaders stopped by Jon's office each afternoon with updates. On his trips to job sites, Jon observed less lounging and more cooperation among team members. For the first time in many months, Jon stopped trying to arrive to work before everyone else. He didn't feel the need anymore.

NOT IF, BUT WHEN MISTAKES HAPPEN

The call came late, after Jon had gone to sleep. He answered the phone with a groggy, "Hello? Uh-huh. Yeah, OK. What's the address again? OK, I'm on my way."

"What is it? What's wrong?" his wife mumbled, half asleep, as Jon began to dress.

"Main break," was all he said.

"Is everyone OK?" she asked. She had grown accustomed over the years to late-night emergency calls.

"Oh yeah, no one hurt," he explained, pulling on a sweatshirt and his jeans. "Just water."

When Jon arrived at McPherson Avenue, he observed the situation. This was a major water line break that would require hours of labor to restore service to the area. Water had been rushing down the street for some time already. The parking lots were flooded. Although it was early in the morning and still dark outside, police had already barricaded a portion of the street, adjacent to the area of the burst.

"What happened?" he shouted, as Emile crossed the street and approached the area. "Where were you guys working the other day? Wasn't it near here?"

Emile walked over. "Pretty close, yeah," he said, motioning a few feet north from where they stood. Carlos, who had also arrived on site, stood by, but said very little.

"I can't believe this happened," Jon said. He was visibly angry and let a few curse words fly. "I can't believe you guys let this happen," he scolded. "Now we're probably going to have to replace the entire stick."

"Looks like it," Emile replied.

"Is this concrete?" Jon asked.

"Looks like it," Emile replied.

Jon couldn't mask his frustration and cursed under his breath, then began issuing curt directives to Emile, Carlos, and the rest of the crew on site. They moved into action, responding quickly, as he directed them.

When Jon felt the incident was under control, he walked across the street to where Stu and Patrick Lacey, Public Works director, were standing. "You OK there, Jon?" Stu asked. He motioned for Jon to walk with him, and they moved across the street, away from where his crew was working. In a soft voice, Stu told him, "I think we can tone it down a bit. No one was hurt. Who is it who always says, 'It's just water?'"

Jon nodded at Stu and explained he believed the break was related to a repair the crew made a few days earlier, on his direction. He relayed the story about how he instructed Emile, by phone, but probably gave the wrong advice. If he'd known they were dealing with concrete pipes, he would have instructed them differently.

"Did you ask them for their recommendations?" Stu asked.

"They should've told me what they were seeing! It's like they're trying to mess with me. They don't tell me anything. As soon as Emile saw they were dealing with concrete, he should've told me." Jon was starting to get upset.

"Yeah, well, I think you thought *you* knew more than they did. Probably better to have your team give you *their* input, since they were the ones on the scene."

Stu shifted into coach gear. "You are not the team. These guys are. Remember what I told you months ago? I didn't hire you to do the work of four crews. I hired you to *manage* the work of four crews."

Jon nodded, now embarrassed by his behavior, and worried that he insulted Emile and Carlos. He walked over to where Emile, Carlos, and the others were working. No matter that it was now four thirty on a brisk fall morning; despite Jon's inappropriate lashing, the four of them were laughing, whistling, and joking while they worked. Jon hated what he had to do. "Hey, you guys, sorry I was a jerk."

"No worries, boss," Sam said. *Suck up,* Jon thought.

"You got this now?" he asked Emile. If he caused any damage to a relationship, it was between him and Emile.

Emile shrugged, giving a short, "Got it."

"OK, thanks. Come see me when you all get this cleaned up then," he said, as he turned to leave. "Please," he added.

"When all this is done," Emile said, "I'll be taking the guys to lunch. Or dinner. Depending on how long it takes us."

"Right, right, of course," Jon replied. "Let me know if you need me," he offered.

When performance problems occur, look at the role you play in the outcome. The adage didn't mean much to Jon when he first heard it in the Moving into Leadership class, but that changed with the McPherson incident. He thought he was *supposed to tell the crew what to do.* He thought being the boss meant being in control; he thought he was astute to not leave anything up to chance. However, no matter what he did, it seemed like morale on Jon's team was getting lower and lower. They were falling more and more behind in their work.

"Your employees need to be clear on the expectations and the standards, yet be free to achieve results in their own way," the facilitator had said.

Jon remembered challenging the facilitator on the entire premise. He set the goals and expectations. "Yes, that's often true," the facilitator agreed. He determined the quality and standards that must be met. "Yes, no argument here," the facilitator said.

"So why do so many mistakes still happen?" he asked.

"Often, the reason is people still aren't clear on the standards. How many of you have ever given an assignment only to be surprised by what they produced?"

"All the time," exclaimed Barbara. "I think I do a good job of explaining what I want, and then when they bring it to me, I'm like, 'What is this?'"

Many others in the room shared similar experiences of surprise and disappointment when the outcome didn't match their expectation.

"It's so common," the facilitator said, and then she went on to explain that our disappointment isn't because people don't complete tasks, but rather that they don't complete them within a particular time frame or to a specific standard.

"We often assume that our employees know what we want. But that's often the source of the misfires. For example, you asked your team to order polo shirts with Axion's logo on them. You wanted a one-inch logo in the upper left corner of the shirt, and instead you got a six-inch logo on the back. But if you didn't clearly specify the size and location of the logo, how can you be disappointed with their decision?"

The number one reason why performance problems occur, she explained, is that people are not clear on *how* things should be completed (standards, timelines, quality, look, feel, etc.).

For example:

- You were expecting the trench to be dug in under two hours; instead, it took them half a day.
- You wanted a nicely catered tray of assorted cheese and canapés and instead the team ordered Chinese takeout.

"If you think about it," she offered, "clear roles and assignments are a gift. If I, as an employee, am clear on what I'm supposed to do and what the standards are, I can focus my attention on that task and devote my energy to it. If I'm confused about who's doing what and what our time frame is, and I'm wondering what Keith is working on, I focus on the unanswered questions.

"A lot of this is about getting over your need for control," she continued. "As you continue to rise in the ranks of this organization, the breadth and scope of your decision-making will expand. You'll be asked to make even bigger and broader decisions that will affect the future of this organization. But you'll have less opportunity to be involved in minor details and tasks. At some point, you'll have to concede decisions to your team members."

She paused, took a breath, then went on, "You won't be able to focus on the details of how your employees are fulfilling their responsibilities. You'll have to, at some point, trust that your employees are competent and allow them to do their jobs. You're going to have to do a little letting go.

"And when you relinquish control, mistakes are bound to happen. Even so, I recommend that you choose your battles, or rather your concerns, wisely. For example, does it *really* matter the size and location of the logo on the shirts?" she asked. "If not, then let it go."

People in the room were stirring, and the energy was heating up. "Does it *really* matter if you got Chinese instead of canapés?" She gazed around the room, inviting their response. "If not, then let it go!" This time, the room chanted "let it go" with her. Everyone burst into laughter.

"However," again she paused, "if it matters that the trench is completed in two hours," she drew the sentence out, for effect, "then be clear up front about your expectations. If you need a procedure followed, a budget met, a goal achieved, let people know the goals and the expectations.

"I have a feeling that many of you are still handling tasks and making decisions that probably can, or should, be handled by your staff. It's time to let some of these tasks go. Let your employees take on some responsibilities so they can learn and grow. This gives you the opportunity to focus on higher-level responsibilities, such as planning for the future success of your team."

Jon had to consider that the McPherson debacle wasn't the fault of Emile or Carlos. It was his—partly because he gave the wrong directions to his team and partly because he just didn't trust them to work out the problem on their own. He meddled when he didn't need to. He was going to have to 'fess up and apologize to them. Stu was right. He wasn't managing the work of four crews; he was trying to do the work of four crews. He had become a crew of one, and as a result, he was beginning to make poor decisions.

for your consideration

How is Jon's lack of trust impacting his crew? How is his lack of trust impacting his credibility as a leader?

It's inevitable that mistakes happen, but what's important is how we, as leaders, respond and react when things go south. What's your take on how Jon reacted when he arrived at the scene of the water break? How do you suggest Jon go about mending any bridges he's burned as a result of his response to his crew at the McPherson water break incident?

What did you learn from this chapter about setting goals and the importance of communicating clear standards and expectations?

What new struggles is Jon facing as he attempts to delegate responsibility to his team? What can or should he do more of to demonstrate his trust and confidence in his crew?

What are you beginning to discover about the relationship between trust, delegation, and employee development?

chapter 8

Understanding the
Nuances of Conflict

"TODAY WE'LL BE COMPLETING an in-class questionnaire called the Thomas-Kilmann Conflict Mode Instrument,[5] which will help you understand how you deal with disappointment, disagreement, and conflict." The facilitator led the class through the completion and scoring of the questionnaire.

Avery was fascinated by her results using this instrument because it finally gave her some clarity into some of her behaviors. Never one to like arguments or disagreements, Avery was prone to give in or walk away instead of addressing an issue head-on. She found it eye-opening to see the different preferences of her classmates, too. Eddie, from Human Resources, was remarkably like Avery. They both tended to either avoid conflict or accommodate others when tensions ran high. Avery usually accommodated, letting the other party call the shots rather than standing up for herself. "Especially if it's not a big deal," she explained to the class, "it's just easier to let the other person have her way."

"That approach sometimes builds goodwill," the facilitator offered. "However, if you always accommodate others, and rarely speak up and assert your interests or needs, how could that impact you as a leader?"

Avery hadn't thought about how her tendencies to avoid hard conversations or accommodate others affected anyone but herself. "How do you mean?" she asked.

"Well, if there's an issue on your team, your role as a leader is to make sure the problem gets addressed, right?" Avery nodded in agreement.

"I think some of us, me included," the facilitator said, pausing for effect, "are afraid we'll say the wrong thing. Or we'll hurt the other person's feelings or make the issue worse if we say something. To avoid any of this pain, we do nothing, hoping the problem will resolve itself, or we give in to the other party to avoid any sort of confrontation." Avery was silent.

Eddie spoke up. "For me, I just don't know how to have these conversations, so I don't do them at all. I'm afraid I'll mess things up worse."

"Yes, but then what?" the facilitator pressed.

"It's not fair to the rest of the team, is it?" asked Michelle. "I mean if there's an issue, but the leader isn't fixing it, then the leader isn't doing her job. And the team isn't as productive as it could be."

"You run the risk of losing the team's trust if you allow conflicts to fester and don't address them," the facilitator said.

Katy interjected, "I scored pretty high in avoidance," she explained, "but I don't do it because I feel like I'll make things worse. I often need to walk away and consider my point of view on a matter. I need time to think and figure out *where do I stand?* on the issue and *what outcome do I want?* It's really about not jumping the gun and putting a little distance between me and the other party, so I'm calm and thoughtful when we finally do sit down and talk."

The facilitator agreed and offered, "That's really an excellent use of avoidance when faced with a conflict. In fact, when used strategically, walking away gives you time to cool down, plan, and think through an issue. All of these are positive uses of that style of conflict management. As leaders, we're more effective when we're familiar with all of these styles and use them with purpose."

Other colleagues in the room, Michelle and Eva, had a preference for the compel/ compete approach to dealing with difficult situations. For them, speaking up and asserting their needs was easy.

"People will walk all over you if you don't speak up," Eva explained. "I'm not mean about it," she continued, "but no one will know my position if I don't tell them." Eva further described that it was hard to not speak up or assert. "If I have an opinion, you'll hear about it," Eva said, with a glint in her eye.

"Me too!" Michelle chimed in. For them, taking some time to ponder or think things over, as Avery and Eddie were likely to do, seemed ineffective.

The group launched into a discussion about the importance of leaders speaking up and taking a stand. "How else can you advocate for your team if you aren't assertive every once in a while?" Barbara asked.

"Yes, but sometimes, some of you," Eddie was looking around the room and eyeing Jon, Michelle, and Eva as he spoke, "some of y'all don't let others get a word in. It feels like it's always your way or the highway."

"I always thought it was a good thing that people called me 'bossy,'" Eva teased.

"I'm actually thrilled to see two women in the room with high scores in compel/compete," the facilitator shared, "because typically women's scores are lowest in that style. I believe it's important for all of us to be able to respectfully and professionally speak up and assert our positions and our needs. As Barbara pointed out, our role as a leader requires that we sometimes take a firm stand. How we do that is what we'll discuss a bit later."

The group continued the discussion about the importance of using different approaches to different situations. They agreed that, when you want your team excited and engaged, collaboration is a good approach because all voices can be heard. But because it takes longer, it's not a good approach when time is of the essence or options are limited. "No need to collaborate when there's a fire, huh?" Barbara joked.

Compromise, the group learned, also brings multiple parties together to develop new solutions, but it takes time. And often all parties are asked to give up something to get something.

"I feel like all I do is compromise," Wes said. In fact, compromise was Wesley's highest score on his assessment. The facilitator, looking over Wes's shoulder at his scores, added, "I'll bet while you're working with a group to reach a compromise, you get so fed up with how long it's taking that you just cave and let others decide." Wes was a little surprised, but the facilitator showed how his two highest scores—first, compromise, and then, accommodation—might lead to that sort of pattern. "I never realized it," Wes said, "but I guess that's my tendency, yes."

Jon remained quiet during the morning's discussion. The topic landed too close for comfort for him, given the recent incident when he lost his cool. The assessment gave words to how he typically dealt with disappointment. His highest score fell in the compel/compete category, followed by avoidance, and then more moderate scores in collaboration and compromise. His lowest score was in accommodation. This meant, according to the facilitator, that Jon was less likely to consider others' ideas or give in to others' approaches. Offering an interpretation of his style when handling conflict, the facilitator suggested that Jon tends to be the driver.

"Your two highest scores, Jon, are compel/compete and avoidance, which fall low on the cooperation scale. It's likely when you're trying to convince someone to go along with your idea, you probably speak directly and with energy behind your words. You may not always seek out the other party's point of view." The facilitator looked for Jon's reaction, and then asked, "Is that pretty close?"

"Probably" he replied, "I guess I tend to either fly off the handle or not talk about things. That's at least how my wife would describe it."

"I have never seen you avoid any conflict, Jon," Barbara challenged. Out of the participants in the class, she had the longest work history with him.

Jon smiled. "Yeah, it's true. My team will tell ya; I tend to call the shots."

Moving the dialogue forward, the facilitator encouraged the class members to reflect on their lowest scores. "Your low scores," the facilitator described, "are those styles you rarely use. What impact, do you suppose, does it have on your team if you rarely avoid a conflict?" It took the class a minute to work through what she was asking. "In other words," the facilitator continued, realizing the original question was not worded well, "if I am always asserting, always speaking up, and never walking away to think through my position, how might I come across to my team?"

This time, a few participants seemed to understand the facilitator's train of thought. "I think what you're asking," Eddie proposed, "is how effective am I as a leader if I never back down."

The facilitator nodded and looked around the room. "Yes," she said. "Yes. That's the idea. Or if you never allow others to bring ideas or have their way."

"Your team might feel as though there's no sense in discussing things with you, if you're always calling the shots," Brad chimed in. "They probably just go along to get along."

"Interesting point, Brad," the facilitator replied. "You might think people agree, but they're really just giving up on engaging with you."

"My guys are happy just having jobs," Jon said, in a deadpan tone.

The facilitator pivoted. "A leader who rarely accommodates may create feelings of helplessness, as in, 'We never have a say.'

"Let's use someone else as an example," the facilitator continued, turning to Avery and asking, "If I may?" Avery nodded. "Avery's highest preference is to avoid conflict. Rather than speak up and address an issue in the moment, Avery may tend to let things go unresolved. Her lowest score is for compel/compete. If Avery rarely asserts her opinions or asserts on behalf of her team, how might her team come to view her?"

The group offered several suggestions, including "Her team may begin to believe that she's not tough enough," and "Her team may see her back down and think she's incompetent if she doesn't speak up."

"The point," the facilitator clarified, "is for us to build competence in these different styles so we're more well-rounded and comfortable with applying them. As leaders, we can't always live in our comfort zones. We must do the work that's in the best interest of our team or the organization. That sometimes will make us uncomfortable."

After a full morning of discussion and self-reflection, the facilitator dismissed the class for lunch. The morning conversation had been engaging, and the group was finally developing a level of comfort with each other.

Jon reflected over his lunch break. He always thought he was supposed to keep everyone in line so no mistakes were made. Call him direct, or call him plain bossy, but it was natural for him to tell people what to do, when to do it, and how. And he got results. His crew rarely disagreed with him, and normally Jon wouldn't think twice about that, but now he was wondering if his hard-driving approach was a problem. More and more people were calling in sick. Emile had put in a transfer to work for another division. He was concerned that Carlos was unhappy. And after his most recent outburst, Jon knew he burned bridges with some of the others. There was little joking, and an uncomfortable silence had returned to the team. He wasn't sure how to build energy and trust in the team and, until now, hadn't considered altering his approach. Without realizing it, Jon gained insight into one of his blind spots which resulted in a streak of insight.

In the Moving into Leadership workshop, the facilitator had explained that we all have blind spots. "You know, those aspects about ourselves that we're not aware of, but everyone else is? Others notice these behaviors, but we're blind to them. Whether it's something positive about ourselves or something we should considering changing, if we're lucky, someone gives us feedback about our blind spots."

I guess I've created an obedient team, but not necessarily a happy one, he thought. And his obedient crews weren't necessarily more productive, either. Before the start of the afternoon session, Jon pulled the facilitator aside. In a subdued tone, he confessed, "You know that accommodation thing we were talking about this morning?"

"I do," the facilitator acknowledged.

"My wife," he continued, with a big grin, "she says I don't do that, either." He was laughing, but the facilitator could tell he was serious in a way.

"I wonder," she asked, "if you were to ease up a bit and let some of the crew members call the shots once in a while, how do you think that might go over with the team?"

"I don't know," he said.

Jon took a slow breath. He didn't want to admit the extent of his outburst at McPherson Avenue, so he simply said, "I don't do very well when mistakes happen."

"What do you mean?" she asked.

"Let's just say I didn't respond the way I should have in the heat of the moment."

The facilitator nodded, as if to console him. "I see. Well," her voice trailed off, then began again, "you know, maybe the rest of the group could also benefit from talking about this. The reality is mistakes are going to happen, whether by you or someone on your team. But what's important is how we deal with them, and," she paused again, gauging Jon's demeanor, "how we reconcile when we don't handle them well. Let's bring this up to the group, as I bet others have similar concerns." Jon nodded and returned to his seat. The facilitator began.

"Jon and I were having an interesting conversation during the break, and I want to ask the rest of you, what's it like for someone to report a mistake to you?"

Michelle was the first to speak up. "I'm pretty straightforward and tell it like it is. Was it a stupid mistake or something that could've been avoided? I'm probably going to tell them so."

"That's that competitive style of yours," the facilitator explained. "And I know you're far more diplomatic than that." She smiled, survey-ing the room. "How about the rest of you? Are you able to stay calm and treat the event as a learning opportunity? Do you get frustrated or angry, insisting that the mistake be rectified immediately? Or do you retaliate in some fashion after the mistake has been cleaned up? Or do you forgive them and move on?"

She regained her focus and continued, "If employees fear they'll be disciplined if they make mistakes, they may be reluctant to report them. And we don't want that. We want our employees to feel comfortable bringing mistakes or problems to us, so we can solve the problems, or learn from the mistakes."

"I'm probably pretty calm about it," Avery shared.

Wes said, "I am the first to admit that I'm a perfectionist and I don't like mistakes. That's not realistic, I know."

"Right," replied the facilitator, "I think we all must concede that mistakes are inevitable. In fact, aren't they the catalyst for learning? I bet if we took time and each replayed a big ol' mistake we made in our past, we'd also discover that we learned something from it.

"What if someone makes a mistake, but it catches you off guard, and you don't respond well? What's the best course of action then?" The facilitator was asking specifically for Jon's benefit, to see if he could gain some wisdom from his peers.

"I think you just have to say 'I'm sorry' and ask for a do-over," Barbara offered.

"Is that realistic?" asked Eva. "I don't want my employees to think I'm weak."

"What will they think of you if you don't apologize when you're acting like a jerk?" asked Wes.

The room went silent.

The facilitator brought the room back. "I think it's wise to know ourselves and be able to manage our reactions when things go south. Because it will happen on your watch. And people—your employees, your boss, your boss's boss, your colleagues—will watch to see how you react. It's awfully hard to redeem yourself as a professional when you've flown off the handle over a minor issue. But it can be done," she stated, giving a compassionate glance toward Jon.

"Never be ashamed or afraid of admitting when you're wrong or have made a mistake. You're human. Be forgiving toward yourself and to those who make mistakes. Learn from them—together—and then move on."

It was a heavy topic that drained the energy from the group, so the facilitator dismissed them for a break. When they returned, they spent the afternoon discussing the qualities and characteristics of each of the conflict styles (Kilmann n.d.). The facilitator helped the group explore the different styles more deeply. They created a diagram that looked something like this:

COMPEL/COMPETE

SOUNDS LIKE:

"Here's what I'm thinking."

"My primary concern is _____."

"I can't get behind that."

"I am ..."

"I'll need to see ..."

BEHAVIORS: Clear articulation. Rephrase your statement. No fuzzy language! Concise statements.

BENEFITS: People are clear on your interests, needs, and concerns. Creates clarity. Establishes boundaries. Clarifies expectations.

DOWNSIDE: Others may interpret you as bossy, unreasonable, commanding. Drill sergeant. If overused, you may be perceived as disinterested in others, uncaring, inflexible, and egotistical.

AVOIDANCE

SOUNDS LIKE:

"I'm not sure where I'm at on this yet. Let me have the evening to think about it."

"I'll get back to you ..."

"Can we talk tomorrow?"

BEHAVIORS: Silence. Walk away. Listen to all sides. Wait to respond. Organize your thoughts. Write out response.

BENEFITS: Time to cool down! Understand your own feelings and position. Assess your interests.

DOWNSIDE: May create distrust. If overused, you can come across as incompetent or disinterested in others and their success. Problems may go unresolved, creating resentment. Problems may become bigger.

COLLABORATION

SOUNDS LIKE:

"Let's get everyone's concerns on the table."

"I'd like to hear from everyone on this."

"What can we work out?"

"What do we have in common? Where are we sideways?"

BEHAVIORS: Listen. Openly share position and point of view. Ask open-ended questions. Check for understanding. Paraphrase to check for understanding.

BENEFITS: Builds engagement. Agreements are solid because all contributed. Creates win-win outcome. Since everyone contributed, hard to sabotage. Builds strong agreements.

DOWNSIDE: Takes time! Takes energy. Can't be used all the time or people will think you can't decide on your own. Not every situation calls for collaboration.

ACCOMMODATION

SOUNDS LIKE:

"Whatever you think is best ..."

"I like your idea. Go for it."

"I'll go along with you."

"What are your ideas? That sounds good."

BEHAVIORS: Listen. Ask for input. Ask for ideas.

BENEFITS: Creates goodwill. People feel their ideas are valued. Frees you up to handle more pressing concerns. Not everything has to be solved by you. Builds competence in others.

DOWNSIDE: If overused, you can appear apathetic or uncaring. People may begin to take advantage of you. People may stop asking you!

COMPROMISE

SOUNDS LIKE:

"Here's what I'm willing to do."

"Are you willing to concede to ...?"

"What can we each agree on?"

BEHAVIORS: Listen. Paraphrase others' statements for clarity. Ask open-ended questions. Ask follow-up questions. Use mechanisms to engage all participants, such as live polling, index cards, whiteboards, etc. Round tables for discussion. Face-to-face discussions.

BENEFITS: Builds strong agreements. Creates goodwill. Demonstrates cooperation.

DOWNSIDE: Takes time! Lots of energy to get and keep everyone talking. If people are passionate about their side, may not work. Both parties give up something to reach agreement.

With a deeper understanding of each style, the group spent the rest of the afternoon on practical tips for speaking up respectfully and holding what the facilitator called "productive conversations."

"How do you feel about sitting down and discussing a problem with an employee or a colleague, or even your boss?" the facilitator asked.

"Well, clearly I will just hope they figure out the problem on their own and fix it," Eddie joked.

"Me too," Avery chimed in, reinforcing her disdain for confrontation.

"How about some of the rest of you?" the facilitator asked.

"I just talk to the person if there's an issue. Let's get it out in the open," Barbara said. Many others agreed with Barbara and shared that, while it's difficult sometimes to deliver bad news or tell people they're not measuring up, their consensus was "tell people the truth."

"Precisely," the facilitator agreed. "But sometimes it's easier said than done. Let's look at some simple things we all can do to make sure these conversations are productive for all parties involved."

HOLDING CONVERSATIONS, NOT CONFRONTATIONS

The group began discussing why so many of us dread conversations dealing with emotionally charged topics.

"How many of you feel comfortable sharing difficult news with an employee?" the facilitator asked the class. Very few hands went up.

"Why do so many of us tend to avoid these conversations?"

"I don't know," offered Wes. "In my experience, I've always said the wrong thing. Or said it in the wrong way, and it's upset the other person."

"I know what you mean," said Eddie. "I find that I beat around the bush to try to soften the message, so I never really say what I want or need to say."

"It's like you hope the other person figures it out if you stammer long enough," Eva contributed.

"I just don't want to hurt the other person's feelings," Eddie said, "or say something the wrong way. I've had that blow up on me in the past with someone running out of my office, crying and upset. It's not a good feeling for either of us."

"And yet, as leaders," the facilitator said, "if there's an issue that's affecting an employee, or the team, it's our obligation to address it."

"I just say it like it is," said Michelle, at which most of the room laughed and agreed that, indeed, that's how she would approach it. With her competitive drive and forceful personality, she is not likely to hedge an issue.

"Can I just call Michelle to handle these conversations for me?" Eddie teased.

"I think perhaps if there's a happy medium," suggested the facilitator, "where we can all be ourselves, yet address the issue respectfully and with kindness, that would be ideal. In their classic work, *Crucial Conversations*, Joseph Grenny and Kerry Patterson[6] offer some basic skills we can use when holding conversations that may be considered sensitive or challenging."

"I never want people to feel cornered or captured by me when I talk to them," said Eva.

"An excellent point, Eva," replied the facilitator. "In fact, what's necessary to create an environment that feels comfortable when you talk to your employees?"

The group brainstormed and shared various ideas about how to manage the space so the energy feels welcoming and positive, regardless of the purpose of the conversation.

"One thing I learned by reading *Crucial Conversations*," shared

Eva, "is to be clear about the purpose of the conversation."

"I remember being called into the boss's office once," Wes recalled, "and I knew immediately it was bad news. He couldn't look me in the eye, fidgeted in his chair, went around and around in circles before finally blurting out 'You have to go.' I asked him, 'Go where?'"

The class erupted in laughter.

"Wes, I'm so sorry to hear about that experience," the facilitator said. "It's so important to be clear on the purpose of your conversation, and, in a business setting such as ours, when we meet with employees to discuss an issue, it's only because we have a good business reason to do so."

"What do you mean? Can you give me an example?" Avery asked.

"Yes, of course. If you have an analyst who is making numerous mistakes that are negatively impacting the rest of the team, that would be an issue that should be brought to the employee's attention," the facilitator explained.

"In the lab," Barbara interjected, "technicians have the freedom to analyze samples in whatever order they wish. It isn't an issue unless or until it creates a significant mistake that affects our day-end results."

"Good example, Barbara," replied the facilitator. "You'll lose credibility if you bring issues to employees that aren't negatively impacting your team. For example, issues such as when they go to lunch, or the order in which they complete tasks. Unless it negatively impacts the organization, or the team, these are details that are not necessarily relevant to work outcomes."

"On my team," Jon finally pitched in, "there's the right way, the wrong way, and my way. And my way *is* the right way."

"Oh Jon," Barbara scolded.

"Actually," the facilitator said, "let's talk about that. 'Because I said so' isn't a business reason. You'll lose credibility if you're expecting people to do things your way, just because you're the boss and you say so. Remember, if there's a genuine deficiency, a potential safety issue, or a lack of skill that's not producing results, we owe it to our team, and the organization, to bring it to the employee's attention so he or she can address the issue. But if you want your employees to do things in a particular way 'just because,' then … well, that's not a compelling reason.

"There are a few key points I want you to keep in mind whenever you need to bring an issue to an employee's attention. First:

1. Concisely explain to the employee the behavior that you want to address and why the behavior is an issue.
2. Seek to understand the employee's side of the situation. You may learn that there are good reasons for the employee's work product, conduct, or situation.
3. Be prepared, however, to explain why and how you need the behavior to change.
4. Allow the employee to change or solve the issue.
5. If necessary, provide any resources or support to help address the issue.

And finally,

6. Always approach these discussions as conversations, and not confrontations.

"Remember, if you've developed trusting relationships with your employees, you and your team members can easily work together to solve any sort of problem that arises. If you're advocating for your employees, you'll first give them the benefit of the doubt. There is so much happening in the workplace—and in your employees' lives—that you may not know about. Use these conversations as discovery sessions. Find out what's going on!"

Conflict comes in many different shapes and forms and is an inevitable aspect of our lives. What are some examples of different types of conflict that you experience on a daily basis? Are some types of conflict easier or more difficult for you to deal with? Why or why not?

What impact do you believe unresolved conflict can have on a team? What do you believe is a leader's role when it comes to managing conflict on a team (or in an organization)?

Are you aware of your attitudes and perspective toward conflict? What is your preferred conflict style?

Give an example of a time when you stepped outside of your preferred conflict style (e.g., confronted someone when you would have preferred to simply ignore the conflict or walk away). What did you do differently in this situation? What was the outcome, and to what do you attribute that outcome?

What conflict resolution skills do you need to further develop?

chapter 9

THE PROBLEM PERFORMER
AND THE IMPORTANCE OF
DOCUMENTATION

DESPITE HER ADMITTED PREFERENCE to avoid confrontation, another payroll mistake was Avery's final straw. She marched over to inform HR that she needed to let Dave go. Her Human Resources liaison, Lisa Hale, listened as Avery vented her dissatisfaction with his overall performance and then described the most recent, egregious mistake that clinched it for her.

Dave's never been a good fit since he started, Avery thought, mentally adding to her list of justifications to let him go.

Lisa interrupted her thoughts, "Can I see your notes?" Her notes. Her notes? Avery confessed, "I haven't been keeping notes on my employees, because most of them do a really good job for me. It's just

Dave. He hasn't been working out."

"Oh," Lisa said, not really hiding her disappointment. "That's OK. How long has Dave been here?"

"Almost a year," Avery replied.

"Perfect," said Lisa. "Let's pull up his six-month performance review."

With a few clicks of her mouse, Lisa brought up Dave's performance review, conducted a few months earlier.

"Hmmm. Well, according to the review you submitted, it appears he met expectations to pass his six-month probationary review. How long has this problem with his performance been going on?"

"I'd say it was shortly after he began. At first, he seemed eager and motivated, but it was short-lived. I've tried to help him along, but he never really seemed very committed to the work." Avery thought back to the change in Dave's demeanor shortly after he began working for her. He took lunches at odd times and didn't seem to have the spark that she thought he would bring. And mistakes! "He makes loads of mistakes," she continued. "The most recent mistake set everyone in Payroll back a good two days as we re-entered and corrected his coding errors."

"I see," Lisa said. "Well, how about your notes from your meetings with him? If you've been talking to him about his performance, we can reference some of those meetings to put together at least a formal Performance Improvement Plan."

Embarrassed, Avery just shook her head, acknowledging that she had no notes, no records, no documentation. There had been no "formal meetings," just brief hallway conversations asking him to pay better attention to details. (*And some sharp looks*, Avery recalled).

An unsettling feeling began to sweep over her. Without documentation outlining Dave's pattern of poor performance, she began to realize she couldn't demonstrate there was a problem.

If it isn't documented, it didn't happen.

Lisa told her, without documentation, there's no proof of what Dave's done or hasn't done, and there's no record of what Avery's done to try to help him improve. The documentation on file with the organization showed that Dave actually "met expectations" in the job for the past few months, because it recorded satisfactory performance. In fact, the documentation supported retaining Dave, not terminating him.

"At this point," Lisa explained, "I'm afraid we just don't have any justification to substantiate a termination. I'll recommend that you first schedule a formal meeting with Dave. At this meeting, make sure you clearly explain that his work product is not meeting expectations and that you are putting him on formal notice that he must improve or be subject to Axion's disciplinary process."

Avery started to get a bit nervous. She asked for a piece of paper and began to take notes.

"OK, so first call a meeting and let him know that this is a formal meeting?" she asked, seeking to clarify.

"Yes," Lisa replied. "Make sure you document the details of this first meeting. Make sure he understands what he's doing or not doing and what he needs to do to improve.

"Document the outcome of the meeting," Lisa explained. "And note if he's agreeable to improving. If he's unaware there's a problem, this first meeting will serve as notice." She paused to allow Avery to catch up with her notes. "Next," she continued, "you must begin to document any problems from this point forward. It may be that just simply calling this to his attention and telling him you are formally putting him on notice will do the trick.

"As a matter of fact," Lisa added, "you should be keeping documentation for all your employees. Documentation can't just be for one person; that can lead to a claim of discrimination or retaliation. Documentation isn't just a nicety; it's a necessity. Begin today to create documentation for all your employees."

"Even though Sandy's just part-time?" Avery asked.

"Yes. And I recommend you set up regular performance meetings with each of them. Meet with each of them and take notes on progress and how they're doing. Don't just capture problems. Make sure you're noting the good things they do as well.

"And are you keeping notes in the online portal?" Lisa asked. Axion had a robust performance evaluation system where performance reviews were posted by supervisors. Avery was embarrassed she logged into the system only when she absolutely had to. She knew little about its features.

After her meeting with Lisa, Avery immediately went back to her office and began to set up a formal system for documenting the performance of each employee. She set up electronic folders on her computer for each person, with subfolders labeled for the current year. Feeling ambitious, she went ahead and created subfolders for the next two years.

"Good to be prepared," she reasoned.

She logged into Axion's online portal system used for annual performance reviews, as Lisa suggested, and dug into the many chat portals and documentation features. *I had no idea any of this was available,* she thought.

On her lunch break, she headed out to a discount store and picked up two spiral notebooks for each employee—one for this year and, again to be prepared, one to have on hand for the following year. Back in her office, she labeled each notebook for each employee, then placed each in a basket labeled just for them. She lined the baskets up on the credenza behind her, for easy access.

Next, she turned to her electronic calendar, scanning her schedule to find an hour to meet with Dave. The earliest was tomorrow, and she sent out an electronic invite for a meeting at nine:

"Hi Dave. I'd like for us to meet tomorrow to go over some of your job duties and discuss any issues. See you tomorrow! —Avery."

The next morning, Avery was nervous about her meeting with Dave. After all, hard conversations were not her forte. She spent the prior evening reviewing her notes from the Moving into Leadership session when they covered the conflict style assessment. She replayed the advice Lisa gave her the day before about how to handle this meeting, such as "Be aware of your intention with this meeting, Avery. Is your goal to help Dave or punish him? If you want to be able to keep him in his job, then the tone of your meeting should be interested and helpful. You'll want to find out where and how he may be struggling."

"He was probably nervous last night, too. I should have told him the purpose of the meeting," she scolded herself. "He was probably more nervous than I am about meeting with me this morning." She chastised herself for yet another leadership failing. *Mental note: One, don't put off these conversations. Two, don't freak out your employees. Three, if you would have these conversations sooner, you wouldn't have to freak out your employees.* She pledged, *Next time I won't put off these things.*

The truth was Avery liked Dave. He was easygoing and had a helpful disposition. He got along with everyone and, while he was a bit of a jokester, it wasn't inappropriate humor but the kind that made everyone cheery and happy. She didn't want to see him fail. But she also needed things to turn around. He continually makes mistakes. *This isn't rocket science,* she lamented.

Her thoughts were interrupted by the knock at her partially open door. "Dave!" she said, motioning him in with her hand. "Come on in. Thank you for stopping in first thing this morning."

"Sure," Dave replied, with a bit of hesitancy. Dave didn't quite understand why he was being brought into the boss's office first thing in the morning. He took the seat across from Avery.

"I really appreciate you stopping in, Dave." she began. "There are some things I want to go over with you, and I also just want to check in with you to see how things are going from your perspective."

Dave began to speak, but Avery continued. "As you probably figured out, there were some pretty big goofs on the last payroll run that cost us a lot of time. I'm wondering if you need a bit more time and training on Wynsome? Or if it's the difference between terminations and additions that's confusing? I'm seeing lots of errors and mistakes happening, and the errors from last week's payroll run cost us a lot of time."

"Um, yeah, some more training would be pretty helpful. No one explained anything about how to compensate for shift differentials. In fact, last week was the first time I'd ever entered payroll for Operations."

"The shift differentials for Operations can sometimes be really confusing," she agreed. Dave looked relieved by her understanding. "Who trained you on them?" she asked.

"No one," he replied.

"Did Lindsay train you on overtime codes?" she asked.

He shook his head.

"Pay adjustments?"

Again, he shook his head "no."

Avery leaned back in her chair and sighed loudly. "Dave, I'm afraid I owe you a big apology," she said. "Apparently, I've been operating under the assumption that you've received training about certain procedures and processes and functions. But it's clear you haven't."

"I've tried my best to pick up on things as I go," he responded, "but there are a lot of custom procedures here that has made it difficult. Alice and Lindsay help whenever I ask, but I also know that answering my questions takes them away from their own work. I've had to figure out some things on my own, which takes a bit longer. And apparently results in mistakes."

"I see," said Avery, "which is why I'm speaking with you now. Only now I'm realizing I'm the one to blame here. I never fully took the time to follow up to make sure you were on track, did I?"

"I think a big part of the issue," Dave continued, "is I've been learning so many variations that it's a little confusing."

"Dave, what else is missing for you? What else would be helpful for you so we can turn this around together and you can feel competent in your work?"

Avery listened as Dave spoke openly about his lack of training and a feeling of isolation within the team.

"I want us to try to come up with a game plan together," Avery said. "What do you think would be helpful for you? What do you need from me?"

They both decided to sign Dave up for a few focused training sessions. "Training is always a good idea," Avery contended. Concluding that Dave needed more one-on-one time with Avery, they agreed to a weekly meeting each Thursday at nine to discuss progress, problems, and issues. Thursday, they reasoned, gave Dave time to make progress, but also an opportunity to make any course corrections before the end of the week.

After he left, Avery was relieved by the conversation, because they were able to work through so much and still end on good terms. She was also sobered by the fact that she was a key player in the problem. *Not a key player—the key player*, she thought. Dave was far from lazy, and in fact showed tremendous integrity and tenacity by trying to figure things out on his own. He never complained, which, as Avery thought, *is both a positive and a negative. From now on, he'll hopefully be more willing to ask questions and talk about problems with me so we can correct them early.*

Avery didn't take enough initiative to make sure Dave was properly trained and keyed-in to the goals and expectations of her department. She didn't clearly outline his job duties and expectations, didn't provide the right training, and didn't follow up with him to make sure he was on track. So Avery, not Dave, was at fault. She committed to rectify the problem.

Come to think about it, she reflected, *if I would've been here on his first day, a lot of this could have been avoided.* She walked to her whiteboard and wrote a reminder to herself: "Create onboarding program for new employees." This orientation program, she decided, would properly introduce new team members to the organization; give them a tiered introduction to the tasks and responsibilities of the job; and provide plenty of coaching, training, and oversight. *The next new employee will be set up for success, not failure,* she vowed.

Turning to her computer, she clicked "accept" to the weekly meeting invitation Dave had already sent her. She pulled down the notebook dedicated to Dave Wilson and began to jot notes about today's meeting.

for your consideration

It's very common for supervisors to forego documenting employee performance, unless and until a problem occurs. However, as this chapter illustrates, it's best to maintain regular documentation for each employee. How does regular documentation benefit the employee, the team, and the organization?

What does Avery discover about the root source of Dave's performance problems?

What did you learn from this chapter about the elements of effective documentation?

How would you assess your comfort level with documentation and with conducting productive conversations around important or sensitive topics? What skills do you need to improve to be more effective?

chapter 10

WHEN THINGS GO SOUTH: ADDRESSING PERFORMANCE ISSUES AND CONDUCTING PRODUCTIVE CONVERSATIONS

AVERY WAS BEGINNING TO UNDERSTAND that conflict takes many different shapes and forms: from a simple misunderstanding that transpired because she was communicating strictly by email, to an upset customer lashing out at one of her support agents, to an entire board of directors who openly argue and disagree with each other.

Over the past few months, Avery noticed a conflict between two of her employees, Shannon Elliott and Brian Graser. *I have no idea why they don't like each other,* she thought, *but I hope they work it out.* Their rift had become more noticeable and uncomfortable. As of last week,

Avery heard through the grapevine that they are no longer speaking, and Shannon has refused to work with Brian.

Unfortunately (or fortunately, depending on how you looked at it), Avery was scheduled for a much-anticipated vacation to Portugal, a trip she and her wife had been planning for some time. Rather than have a conversation with them before she left, Avery took off for vacation, hoping that the two of them would smooth things over while she was gone.

Upon her return, the glow from Avery's amazing trek to Portugal didn't last long. She soon learned that things had escalated from bad to toxic, and in a contemporary version of the Jets versus the Sharks, team members began to take sides. They either stood with "Shannon/Jets" or "Brian/Sharks."

Avery had no choice but to sit down and talk with the two employees to end the bickering and get them working productively together again. Not quite sure how to deal with the situation, Avery once again reached out to Lisa, in HR, for advice.

"How long has this been going on?" Lisa asked.

"For several weeks," Avery replied, and then fibbing, added, "I didn't have time to deal with it before I left for vacation, and things have apparently escalated while I was gone."

Of course, it wasn't that Avery didn't have the opportunity to address the issue before she left. She just didn't want to because Avery, like so many of us, prefers that everyone gets along. Dealing with confrontation or holding difficult conversations is not her favorite thing to do.

"I think you're going to have to meet with each of them and find out each side of the story," Lisa recommended. Avery agreed, reluctantly, to do so and went back to her office to schedule meetings with both for the following day. She already had a good idea that the issue stemmed from their competitive natures. Shannon felt Brian was taking too much credit for work he did on a water usage report commissioned by the board of directors. Avery also knew that Brian put significant effort into translating some of the hard data for that report into trend analyses that could be applied to other projects. While Shannon had researched and collected most of the data, it was Brian who made sense of it and presented it in a user-friendly format. Avery wasn't quite sure exactly where things went off track between these two talented analysts.

Brian immediately replied to Avery's request and agreed to a meeting at nine the next morning. Avery waited until close of business and still had not received Shannon's reply.

She wasn't quite sure what to expect from either Brian or Shannon. They were both pleasant and professional around her. But when they were forced to be in the same environment, the energy was tense and strained. Their rift had become an elephant in the room that everyone tiptoed around. Avery didn't know if she could smooth this over, but she knew she had to try, because she couldn't have two employees not talking or creating discord within the team. It was creating unnecessary tension within the entire team and slowing productivity.

In the Moving into Leadership program, Avery was learning that her role wasn't so much to eradicate conflict, because it's ever-present in one shape or another, but rather to create the space where people can talk through their differences to find common ground, compromise, or agreement. In many ways, robust conversations, which carry with them a level of conflict, can be energizing and can spark new ideas. As Michelle explained in their last session, "You can't really innovate or achieve a new level in your life if you never get passionate and openly express yourself!"

When used appropriately, conflict serves such a purpose, but when left unchecked, as in Avery's predicament, conflict becomes a hinderance. Avery realized she would have to take an active role in managing their conflict, which made her very uncomfortable. Maybe it would just be a matter of setting some simple boundaries for Brian and Shannon, as in, "You don't have to like each other, but you do have to work respectfully with each other." But her fear was she would have to enforce expectations about their behaviors while at work. She hoped for the former outcome, for everyone's sake.

The irony didn't escape her, though. Avery realized that she shouldn't have put off talking to Brian and Shannon. *This is yet another example of my avoidance tendencies! Why did I let this go on for so long?* Annoyed at herself for ignoring the pledge she made just weeks before, Avery took a long, slow breath and tried to figure out a game plan for how to proceed. She wasn't sure how or if she could resolve it, but she knew something had to be done.

That night, she tried to push the issue out of her mind, telling herself, *I'm not going to make this into a big deal. I'm just going to tell them both to get along and figure things out.*

Avery arrived early to the office and dug into her inbox. Before long, there was a knock on the door. Avery had lost track of the time.

"Good morning," Brian offered. He took the seat across from her desk. "How was your trip?" he asked.

"It was amazing!" she said, eager to share details about it. She told a funny story about missing a ferry and getting stranded by herself at a tourist resort. Then, realizing she was drifting off point, she shifted the conversation, and her tone, back to the topic at hand. "I'd love to go on and on about it, but ..." She paused, then continued. "I want to talk with you. About what's been going on with you and Shannon. I heard things got a bit dicey while I was gone."

Brian, a bit surprised by the turn in the conversation, began to stammer, "Well, I don't really think it's my ..."

Avery didn't give him a chance to continue, but instead interrupted, "I don't know what the issue is, Brian, but I really need your help to smooth all this over."

She continued, "I know it's hard, but this rift is getting silly. I don't care what the issue is, but I need it to end."

"If I need to intervene I will," she said flatly, "but I don't want to have to."

Brian had already begun to stand up to leave. "I'll see what I can do, Avery," he said curtly. He turned and left Avery's office without another word.

"Thank you," Avery called after him. "Thank you," she whispered again to herself. She took a deep breath. *Did that go well?* She wondered. She couldn't tell. *I don't think that went well.*

Grabbing her coat, Avery headed outside for a quick walk to capture her thoughts. It was a frigid morning, and she walked briskly, pulling her coat around her tightly. As she walked, she replayed the conversation in her mind, trying to understand how it went downhill. *I think I rushed into that conversation,* she reflected. *No, more like steamrolled over him,* she admitted. *He really didn't have much of a chance to defend himself,* she sighed.

Wishing there were such a thing as actual do-overs, Avery returned to her office, feeling a bit more composed than when she left, and saw an email response from Shannon. Avery immediately replied, asking her to stop by her office as soon as possible.

All these "people issues" were beginning to take a toll on Avery. She hoped her conversation with Shannon would be more productive. There was a quick rap on the door.

"Is this a good time?" Shannon asked.

"Of course. Come in." Avery was nervous to talk with Shannon after the poor outcome she had with Brian. She didn't want to make things worse than they already were! She took a deep breath, and in a voice much softer and lower than usual, said, "Shannon, I need your help. This thing going on between you and Brian has been going on for a while. What is this all about?"

Partly because she was disappointed by the way her conversation with Brian ended and partly because she didn't know what else to say to Shannon, Avery leaned back in her chair and was silent.

Shannon spent a good thirty minutes recounting her frustrations and fears: frustrations about feeling taken for granted and fears about being passed over for the next promotion. Avery had no idea that Shannon was so insecure about her position with the department and was disheartened to hear that she didn't feel as though she was receiving enough positive feedback from Avery to allay her fears of being dispensable.

"So, this really isn't about Brian, is it?" Avery finally asked.

Shannon looked up at the ceiling and shook her head while answering, "No. I guess not."

"So how do we fix this?" Avery asked. "I need you and Brian to become that dynamic duo again, that pair I could always rely on to produce."

All told, they spent a good hour together, with Shannon doing most of the talking and Avery doing most of the listening. Shannon left Avery's office promising to reach out to Brian to make amends and make things right.

Avery knew that she, too, needed to apologize to Brian. The way she handled her conversation with him was completely unprofessional and ineffective.

I need to talk to Brian, she told herself, *and quickly before I do any more damage.* She walked to his office, catching him just as he was leaving for lunch. "Brian, may I apologize to you? I did not handle our earlier conversation well, and I respectfully request a do-over." She gave a meek smile and waited for his response.

Always gracious, Brian accepted her apology, but Avery knew it would take time to restore his trust.

"Of course, Avery," Brian said. "I understand."

Avery asked if they could begin again. "I'd like to hear your side of things, if you'll tell me," she said. "Do you mind if we stay and talk?" Avery hated to keep him from his lunch, but she also didn't want the events of the morning to grow wings and fester.

They sat down in Brian's office, side by side, and, with a bit of coaxing, Brian finally opened up about his frustration with the lack of recognition for his contributions. As she did with Shannon, Avery sat quietly and just listened, as Brian described his attempts to smooth things over with Shannon.

"She just wouldn't have it," he said. He shared his concerns that this rift would negatively impact his ability to be promoted, something he'd been pursuing for several years now. "Before you came on board," he explained, "I was in line for your position." That was a revelation for Avery. He talked for several minutes about his uncertainty about Avery's expectations and whether he was meeting them or not. "It feels sometimes that you have expectations for us, but we're not allowed to know what they are. We just have to guess."

Avery was impressed that he was willing to be so honest and up-front with her about his frustrations and concerns. "I'm grateful for your honesty," she said. She had no idea she wasn't giving Brian enough of her time and input!

"It seems as though we have a couple of issues to address," Avery concluded. "One is how can you and I create more open and honest communication?" Brian smiled in agreement. "And two," she continued, "is how to address the rift between you and Shannon." She told him of Shannon's interest in speaking with him to mend bridges. "I'd like that," Brian said.

With the air a bit lighter, the two of them made plans to speak again the next morning. "Let's you and I figure out a way that we can continue these kinds of conversations," she suggested. "I've kept you long enough; you must be starving," she said, as she stood to leave. "Have a nice lunch. And thanks again for your understanding, Brian."

Avery was surprised by what she learned from her conversations with Shannon and Brian. She knew that, as a leader, she would be called upon to solve many different types of issues. This was her first foray into employee conduct and conflict. Avery was struck by how different her three conversations were. Later, on her drive home, she analyzed the differences.

In her first conversation with Brian, her bias was revealed. *These two are out to get me,* she remembers thinking. She remembers not looking forward to the first conversation with Brian. That sense of dread could have fueled her irritation, which she then took out on him.

Avery recalled a conversation at one of the Moving into Leadership workshops when they were discussing how to conduct difficult conversations. A participant had asked the facilitator, "If we go into a conversation with an employee and we're thinking it will be difficult, then aren't we setting ourselves up to have a difficult conversation?"

The facilitator had replied, "Yes. Yes, you will. If you begin a conversation with a bias or preconceptions, then yes, you *will* set yourself up for a self-fulfilling prophecy."

Indeed, Avery thought, *I was mad at Brian and the situation before I ever spoke to him. And I had a sense the conversation wasn't going to* go well. *So, in fact, it turned into a self-fulfilling prophecy.* It was just as the facilitator cautioned.

She also had convicted Brian before he even spoke! She should have kept an open mind to learn Brian's side of the issue. Avery shook her head and realized just how tricky these sorts of conversations can be.

There was no opportunity for him to share his side of the story. *I did all the talking,* she reflected. Then, realizing what she had done, she laughed to herself. *And I told him what he needed to do to solve his problem!*

What made my conversation with Shannon so different? she wondered. She didn't do much talking; that was certain. In fact, she realized, *I mostly just listened. I was a sounding board.* The same was true for her second go-round with Brian, she realized. *I just gave him the space to vocalize his thoughts and experiences.*

Her most profound realization was the power of not solving their problem for them. *Shannon drew her own conclusions about what needed to happen. She basically solved her own problem.*

Avery felt grateful for these conversations, as she learned a lot about what not to do when discussing sensitive or difficult topics. For example, *I can raise an issue with employees, and help them understand why the issue is a problem, but I don't have to solve their problems for them. If it's their problem, I shouldn't solve it for them. I just need to be the sounding board to help them figure things out on their own.*

But what surprised her the most was what she discovered about her relationship with both. Both Shannon and Brian claimed they weren't getting enough input, feedback, and guidance from her! All these months, she thought she was being helpful by leaving them alone, but instead, they wanted her time, and her attention.

Many revelations happened on that evening's drive home. By the time she pulled into her garage, Avery was humbled by the day's experiences. *I think, for the first time in a long time, I made a difference. I may have taken the long way around to do so, but I think good things happened today.*

She walked into the house, eager for dinner and to decompress after a long day.

What did you notice about the differences between Avery's three conversations? What were some of the techniques she used in her conversations with Brian and Shannon? Were you surprised by the different outcomes each conversation produced? What techniques can you apply the next time you must hold a productive conversation?

What are you discovering about conflict in the workplace and your responsibility, as a leader, when it comes to managing conflict?

What can you, as a leader, gain by engaging with conflict?

chapter 11

YES, ANOTHER MEETING: BUILDING EMPLOYEE ENGAGEMENT

AVERY WAS STRUCK BY THE INFORMATION she gathered from her conversations with Shannon and Brian. And she was certainly enlightened by her meeting with Dave. It made her think, *I'm hearing more and more that people want my time. Maybe Lisa was right in suggesting regular meetings with everyone.*

In the Moving into Leadership program, the group learned that employees are more likely to report higher levels of engagement, satisfaction, and interest in their work when they have time with the boss.[7] Avery wouldn't have guessed this to be true, though, based on the response she received when she announced her idea to her team.

"From now on," she said, "each of you will have a standing, monthly, one-hour meeting with me." The group groaned loudly, partly just to tease her.

"These meetings are our opportunity to discuss everything and anything related to you, your work, and your professional goals. I expect we'll use quite a bit of time to talk about work issues and any challenges you're having. But I also want to get to know about you and your goals so I can better assist you."

Ever fearless to speak her opinion, Lindsay broke the team's silence, "Avery, we're all so busy. This feels like just another burden to add to my plate." Others around the table echoed the sentiment and began to protest.

"I know, I'm busy too!" said Avery. "But I really think if we commit to this, it will save us all time in the long run." She paused to gauge the group's reaction, then continued to build her case. "OK, take last week, for example." Avery reminded the group that Lindsay and Dave each spent hours completing the exact same payroll reconciliation. "Now we also should be catching these duplications in our team meetings, but that's a different issue. I think meeting regularly will help alleviate these kinds of redundancies, and I want us to give this a try."

Avery thought back to what Lisa had told her. "You'll think you can't possibly find time to meet regularly with each of your direct reports, but if you follow this advice, you'll actually save time because you'll improve communication, reduce errors, increase trust, and decrease problems. In fact, you'll discover once you start meeting regularly with each of your direct reports, you'll actually have more time rather than less."

"How can that be?" Avery had challenged.

"Well, think about it," Lisa said. "When you meet on a regular basis, you're more current on the status of projects. If there's an issue with a project, it's likely to come up earlier, rather than later, and it's always easier to solve problems when they're small than when they're huge."

Avery had liked the sound of this advice, and it fit with what she had learned from her experience with Dave. Many of the issues she had encountered with Dave's work could have easily been corrected if she had met with him regularly. And once she began doing so, his work improved by leaps and bounds. He was unstoppable as long as he was clear on procedures and understood the rationale behind them. Lisa had also said, "Regular meetings with each employee force everyone to pay attention.[8] They put everyone on notice, in a way. It's harder to get away with not doing something when you know someone will hold you accountable. I think you'll find everyone will stay current and on top of things more."

Avery remembered that she had nodded in agreement. "You're right, of course, and this is exactly what's happened with Dave. But I'm also discovering so much about our processes and systems—things I never would have known unless Dave and I were digging into things together. It's very revealing."

"I have a feeling if you start this habit of regular meetings, you'll learn even more," Lisa had said.

That's why Avery couldn't help but think that regular meetings would help everyone else on the team. *I can better keep people focused and on track,* she told herself. *And maybe we can better figure out if there's duplication of efforts, or fix other issues affecting our work.*

Avery knew that some of the pushback was premised on fear: fear that they would get more behind in their work and fear of being micromanaged.

Lisa's advice to her was still vivid. "My caution to you, Avery, is don't allow these meetings to get rescheduled or fall off the radar. If you end up meeting with your employees only when there's a problem, the very nature of the meetings will shift from 'checking in' with people to 'checking up' on them. If you're meeting to check up on your employees, you're not partnering with them—you're overseeing them, and that creates a very different feeling for employees."

Heeding Lisa's warning, Avery pressed on, anticipating further pushback from the group. "I also want you to know that this is not about me 'checking up' on you. There's a fine line between checking up and checking in. These meetings are designed to keep you and me current about your work progress and address any issues or challenges you're having, so I can help remove barriers or help you get the resources you need."

Despite a few more protests, Avery held her ground, making it clear "We are trying this." She offered one last edict to the group. "One other thing," Avery looked around the table. "I will commit to be present for these standing appointments with each of you. And my expectation is you will commit, too. Please do not cancel with me at the last minute because you accidentally (she used air quotes) double-booked yourself for our scheduled meeting. Don't space out your meeting with me, and above all, come prepared with questions, progress reports, and things to discuss. I'll be forwarding you all a format to help us initially with these meetings. After we leave today, it will be up to each of you to schedule your time with me. Create a recurring meeting that works best with your schedule—and, of course, for a time that's open on my calendar, too."

"What about vacations?" asked Todd.

"There will be no more vacations," she replied, stone-faced. Then, seeing the look of concern on Todd's face, she quickly corrected her tone. "Just kidding, just kidding," she explained. "We'll work around vacations and anything else that comes up, but I'm hoping that we'll all start to appreciate these meetings."

MEETING MATTERS

True to her nature, Avery designed a checklist to help guide the conversations in her one-on-one meetings. She wanted to make sure she didn't just jump into task mode, so she decided each meeting would begin with "catching up." Then, she reasoned, she could launch into business matters. *After all,* she thought, *there's more to our relationships here than just the work.*

Here was her recommended format for her one-on-one meetings:

Personal stuff:

How are they? What's new in their life?

Check-in on current projects:

1. Are projects on target?
2. Are projects completed?
3. Address any snags or complications with current projects:
   - Set new timelines, if necessary and possible. If not, work together to create a new plan to meet predetermined deadlines.

Check-in on professional goals and needs:
- What are you proud of from the past week?
- Any problems or frustrations you're experiencing?
- Are you adequately challenged at work or overwhelmed?
- Are you working toward your goals?

Feedback:

1. Share at least one positive contribution I observed or witnessed since our last meeting.
2. Share an example of their strengths at work and the value each brings to this team.
3. Address any deficiencies, and discuss next steps.
4. Provide feedback to help improve performance, if necessary.

Feeling satisfied that she had a solid plan in place, she printed out copies of her checklist and stapled a copy inside the front cover of each employee's notebook. She created a shorter outline for the meetings and sent that out to the team as promised.

She looked forward to using her new approach in her first meeting which was with Lindsay, first thing on the following Monday.

"Good morning, Lindsay," Avery said with her cheeriest Monday morning voice. It was a little early for Avery to do the people stuff, but this was when the meeting worked best for Lindsay's schedule, so Avery didn't argue.

"Good morning," Lindsay replied, sliding into the chair across from Avery. "So, how does this work?" she asked.

"Well, I think just like this …," Avery answered, hoping to build some conversational momentum. "How is everything in your world?"

"Good," came the response.

Avery pulled her meeting outline closer to her and glanced over at it. "Anything new in your life?"

"Not really." Lindsay's response made Avery feel as though she were talking to a petulant seventh grader after school.

"OK," Avery persisted. "Well, let's just jump into projects and status updates. How are things going with HR? Making any progress?"

Lindsay dutifully answered Avery's questions, not providing a lot of detail, but not avoiding her questions either. Their meeting ended after only twenty minutes, but Avery was satisfied. She had received an update on the HR payroll report changes and was comfortable with Lindsay's progress in other areas. She wrapped up the meeting with, "Well, for our first meeting, I think it went pretty well. How would you grade it?"

"Fine," said Lindsay.

Undeterred, Avery used one more tool in her toolkit before she released Lindsay back to her workweek. "I wanted to let you know, Lindsay, how grateful I am to have you on my team. You are so good with customers! I've overheard, on several different occasions, you calm down a frustrated supervisor or help an employee understand her paystub. Whenever someone has a question, I know you can help them through it. I'm not sure if you realize what an innate talent that is?"

Lindsay remained fixed in Avery's doorway. "At any rate," Avery continued, "I'm so glad you're on my team, because I can't do what you do." She smiled, but sensed Lindsay was slightly embarrassed, so she offered her an escape. "OK. Well, have a great week, and let me know when we're ready to make decisions with HR."

"OK, thanks," Lindsay said. She started to leave, then turned back around and offered, "I'll let you know what I hear from HR."

That was cool, Avery thought, feeling as though she might have penetrated behind Lindsay's rough exterior. While it was true that Lindsay was effusive and warm with others, it didn't extend to their relationship. She hoped Lindsay heard her feedback as genuine and sincere. Avery jotted the details discussed during their meeting in Lindsay's notebook, making sure to note the positive feedback she shared with her.

The other one-on-one meeting she held that week with Shannon went basically the same as Lindsay's: fairly awkward, a little strained, but overall productive. Avery was satisfied. *Baby steps,* she reminded herself. *We're all learning and adjusting to these meetings.* Except for Dave, with whom she had already met, the others were initially a bit cautious about what they shared. She assured herself that their interactions and conversations would become more relaxed and meaningful as time went on. After lunch on Friday, she looked over the cheat-sheet she had made. She jotted a few notes in the margins to guide her.

Instead of the note to ask "What's new?" she wrote, "Tell me about your weekend." Instead of "Are projects on target?" she wrote, "Tell me about the status of XYZ project" and "What are your plans for_____?"

Avery recalled questions were the focus of one of the Moving into Leadership sessions.

"Performance coaching is one of the most effective methods for achieving employee engagement," the facilitator had said, "and our effectiveness is only as good as the questions we ask." Avery had never considered herself a coach or a mentor but liked the idea of that role rather than "the boss."

"I'm not the boss type," she had shared with her colleague, Mary Jo, "but I can see myself advising and coaching my employees, especially if it's on something I know really well."

"As performance coaches," the facilitator had explained, "we observe our employees and provide useful feedback to help them improve. We help them realize tendencies and talents they might not be aware of. Think about all the things that athletic coaches do, for example."

Working together, the class had discussed the qualities and behaviors of good athletic coaches.

"I remember a college running coach who helped me figure out the slightest shift in my gait, which actually transformed the way I ran. I improved my time so much I won the first race I ran after working with that coach," Eddie explained. His voice, cracking a little, betrayed the long-held emotions about that time in his life.

The facilitator wrote on the whiteboard:

- Good coaches provide helpful/constructive feedback.

"If I wasn't told to swim so many laps every day," Barbara shared, reflecting on her experience on her college swim team, "I never would have learned discipline, which has been so helpful to me in later years."

The facilitator wrote:

- They set standards and goals that help an athlete progress.

"And I hated those daily laps," Barbara confessed. "But I needed someone to push me."

The facilitator wrote:

- Good coaches challenge and push you, often beyond what you think you can do.

It was rare when Jon spoke up and shared in these workshops, but this time he did, telling the group, "My high school football coach was a tough coach, but he was also kind. We knew he cared."

"What did he do that made you know he cared, Jon?" the facilitator had asked.

"I don't know. I think it was because he didn't let us get away with crap. He thought we could do things we never thought possible. He believed we could go to State, and so we worked hard to prove him right. He never gave up on us, or got frustrated, or gave us any indication we were a hopeless case," he paused, "even though we probably were." Jon grinned. "Like, early in the season, when we showed no signs of ever being able to win a game, he didn't say 'OK, well let's just try to get one down.' He always spoke to us as though we were going to win the next game. He believed in us."

The facilitator wrote:

- Good coaches support, encourage and motivate. They don't let you quit.

> Good coaches provide helpful/constructive feedback.
>
> They set standards and goals that help an athlete progress.
>
> Good coaches challenge and push you, often beyond what you think you can do.
>
> Good coaches support, encourage and motivate. They don't let you quit.

To his tablemates, Jon added, "He was cool. He passed away last February, and I went to the funeral. You wouldn't believe all the people who showed up. He touched a lot of kids."

Getting nostalgic, the conversation made Jon also think about Stu, and how similar he is to that high school football coach. Jon was beginning to see how Stu's confidence and faith in him made Jon want to be better.

"And so, as leaders, we use many of the same techniques that any good coach uses. Performance coaches do everything you just identified. We assess our employees. What are they good at and what is getting in their way? We learn about their goals and ambitions. And it's up to us to give them the structure and guidance they need so they can achieve their goals," she said.

"The language we use and the questions we ask are very important," the facilitator advised, "and our most effective tools are listening, asking questions, and observing.

"Consider this scenario," she began. "Cait has asked her employee, Jan, to come to her office. Jan has made numerous mistakes entering data, and Cait wants to ensure that Jan understands the correct fields to populate, the correct options to select under certain circumstances, and the correct way to close out the entry. Which of the following scenarios would you find most effective, and why?"

Scenario A: Cait brings Jan into her office. Jan sits side by side with Cait, looking onto her screen. Cait brings up a screen, and, running through the various fields, demonstrates to Jan the correct process and procedure. She asks, "Any questions?"

Scenario B: Cait begins by saying, "I've noticed a few areas where you've been struggling, and mistakes are consistently made. I want to make sure you're confident with the process, to eliminate any mistakes going forward." Cait asks Jan to "walk me through how you would enter this intake form." Cait observes Jan working, and then asks clarifying questions such as "Which of the top fields can you ignore?" and "Show me which fields you enter first, second, etc."

The class had discussed both scenarios. "In the first scenario," Michelle said, "the supervisor is just showing, or doing it for her. But in the second case, she's asking questions to gauge how much her employee knows. Then she evaluates how her employee works with the database."

"If she keeps asking questions, like in the second version, maybe Jan can figure out her mistake on her own," Keith suggested.

"Good point, Keith," the facilitator noted. "Questions—open-ended questions, probing questions, clarifying questions—these are all tools to help our employees wrestle with information on their own. Questions help us gather input and information.

"As leaders, we need to know what our employees know. We need to know their level of knowledge, their assumptions, and their critical-thinking skills," the facilitator said. "If we don't know what—or how much—our employees know, then how can we feel comfortable letting them make decisions on their own?"

"We can't," Jon interjected. He was referring to an earlier workshop in which he and the facilitator debated the merits of equipping employees with fundamental safety knowledge. During that workshop, she had asked Jon, "Would you feel more comfortable allowing your employees to work independently if you were convinced they knew how to work safely?"

Since that discussion, Jon made safety awareness and safety training one of his core priorities. He leaves each job site he visits and each meeting with his crews with a mandate to "work safe and work smart."

Avery studied the universe of questions the class had created in the Moving into Leadership workshop. Some seemed trite and silly, but others felt useful and helpful. She created a cheat-sheet of open-ended questions to use in her one-on-one meetings:

- What are your recommendations?
- What concerns should I know about?
- How will you proceed?
- What are your options?
- What challenges do you anticipate?
- What resources do you need?
- What did you do well?
- What would you do differently next time?
- What are our strengths moving forward on this project?

The facilitator had continued, "Your employees want your input. They need your constructive feedback in order to improve or achieve new goals."

"I never know what or how to give feedback," Wes admitted. Several others in the workshop nodded in agreement.

FEEDBACK FUNDAMENTALS

"Well, then, let's talk about that," the facilitator suggested.

"Imagine this," the facilitator began. "You're bowling, but the pins you're aiming for are behind a curtain, so you can't see them. You throw the ball down the lane, and can hear the crash of some pins, but you can't see how many pins you laid down or which ones. How long would you continue to bowl without ever knowing how you're doing?"

The class looked a bit surprised by the scenario but played along.

"Well, it wouldn't be very much fun, would it?" asked Michelle.

"I don't know how I could continue to play, because I wouldn't know how to throw my second ball," Avery said. "How can I make adjustments to knock down the remaining pins if I don't know which ones are remaining?"

"Exactly," the facilitator stated. "Exactly. Working without feedback is a little like that bowling scenario—you don't know how you're doing or if you need to make a correction. Feedback is essential for all of us, because it gives us the input we need to make course corrections. Feedback is what we need in order to know what we're doing well or to learn what's not working, so we can adapt or change our behavior. Without feedback, our performance will never improve."

"I see what you mean," Eva said. "There are so many times that I don't hear from my boss. In some way, I want to know 'what am I doing right?' or 'what should I be doing more or less of?' I sometimes feel lost, like I'm bowling blind."

"If we're in this for the organization, and, if we're in this for our team members," the facilitator said, "then I think our employees deserve helpful input. What are they doing that's having a positive impact? Point out those behaviors to them so they know what to keep doing. And if they're doing things that aren't working, we owe it to them to point those out, too. Always remember, people will continue to do what they are positively rewarded for doing."

The facilitator had divided the class into small groups and asked them to brainstorm the essential elements of effective feedback. One group came up with the following list:

- Make it meaningful. The feedback you give me should help me improve or enhance my abilities.
- Be specific. Don't just tell me I'm amazing.
- If I'm doing something wrong, tell me right away. Don't wait six months until my performance review.

Group two came up with this list:

- Give me feedback on something I have control over, e.g., behaviors I can control.
- Give me feedback on what I do well.
- Help me understand the impact of my behavior (when you do this, this happens).
- Be sincere.

Group three's list included:

- Give me feedback so I can improve in ways that are meaningful to me.
- Give me feedback in the moment.
- Be specific, so I know what to keep doing or stop doing.

"These are great lists," the facilitator said, "and they reflect key points we all should remember as leaders. Above all, we all need feedback. And I encourage you, as leaders, to ask your employees to give you feedback, too. What do your employees think you do well? How can you improve to be a more effective leader to them?"

"That feels risky," Michelle admitted.

"It is," the facilitator agreed, "but it's important. It sets an example for the team and demonstrates that you're open to learning and growing. Feedback shouldn't be feared. Feedback becomes feared only when it's personal, or when it's used to punish or make us feel bad."

"Or it feels retaliatory," Eddie contributed.

"Indeed," the facilitator said. "Feedback should feel as though it's a gift, especially if it's given sincerely and with good intentions.

"We all deserve helpful feedback. Please be thinking about how you can provide feedback to your team members to help them develop and grow." And with that the facilitator had concluded their session.

for your consideration

What are you discovering about the benefit of regular one-on-one employee meetings?

What ideas do you now have to transform your one-on-one meetings into productive coaching sessions?

What's your take on the difference between "checking up" on employees and "checking in?" Is there a difference, and if so, why?

What are some of the coaching skills revealed in this chapter? What techniques or coaching approaches can you implement as a leader?

What are you learning about the characteristics of effective feedback?

Have you ever received really helpful feedback? If so, what made it helpful for you? What can you do to make the feedback you give to your team helpful, constructive, and productive?

chapter 12

Focus on Potential within Your Team

IN THE MOVING INTO LEADERSHIP PROGRAM, the class discussed the contention that effective leaders try to catch people doing things right[9]. Jon was one of the first to comment, admitting that initially he had it all backwards.

"I thought I was supposed to keep people from goofing off or goofing up, so I was constantly watching my crew and waiting to catch any little slipup," Jon said. "And when I did catch them, I was all over them like white on rice. I was always just waiting for someone to mess up so I could be the disciplinarian."

If someone on his team stepped up, showed initiative, or offered an idea that was outside the box, Jon would shoot it down. "I come up with the ideas around here," he would brag. If change was going to happen, it was going to come from him. If there were new ways of doing things, it would come from him. It didn't take the crew members long to figure out that, on Jon's team, you "keep your head down and just do what you're told." And since there was little incentive to go above and beyond, Jon's crew focused on maintaining the status quo. There was little innovation or change happening on Jon's crews. They did the work, but without much energy and fanfare.

By contrast, the class learned, the most effective leaders consciously create a culture that rewards innovation and good work by pointing out the behaviors, attitudes, and beliefs that are in alignment with the organization's goals.

"Where do you place your focus at work?" the facilitator asked during one of the final sessions. It was another one of those questions that the group, initially, didn't know how to answer, so she rephrased the question as, "How much of your day is spent with your poor performers versus your star performers?"

"All my employees are rock stars," Keith stated, tongue in cheek.

"Mine too," Michelle agreed.

This was a question that Jon hadn't considered. Where did his time go during the day? He spent a lot of time at job sites, checking on crews, and making sure everything was going as planned. Beyond that, he was either at meetings or at his desk, responding to emails. He offered up a portrait of his typical day. "My day is usually spent in the field, and I spend a lot of time checking in on my teams. Otherwise, it's meetings, meetings, and more meetings."

"And for all of you," asked the facilitator, surveying the group, "are you spending your time finding faults? Or brilliance? It's an important distinction."

Jon thought about this but initially decided it didn't apply to him.

While he was learning to help his employees be successful, his definition of success was "staying within the lines of the job." He wanted to help his employees, but they first had to do things correctly.

That's why he spent so much time with those who needed his help. He was grateful he had so many competent crew members on his team. "Carlos—he's definitely my go-to guy," Jon explained that afternoon over a group lunch with colleagues from the leadership program. "And I can always count on Jimmy and Emile. I never have to worry about them."

But the others, he explained, were still learning, so they needed more of his time and attention. "I wouldn't be doing my job if I didn't correct their mistakes," he reasoned.

"If you focus on exceptional performance and reward initiative, innovation, and ingenuity," the facilitator suggested, "you'll get more of the same. Leaders encourage people to do more of certain productive behaviors and less of other, unproductive behaviors."[10]

"I never thought about it before," Avery admitted, "but I figure my rock stars don't want my feedback or my help. And they probably don't need my encouragement. So, I leave them alone. But it's interesting to think that maybe that's backwards. Maybe I should be calling out, more often, the great work they do for me, so they know I notice. And, that I care."

The discussion was making Jon a little uncomfortable as he realized that he, too, spent far more time with his poor performers and less time with Jimmy or Emile or Carlos. In fact, none of his "star performers" probably even knew they were his star performers!

The next day, as Jon arrived at his office, he was surprised by a visit from Carlos, asking if he had a few minutes.

"You bet," Jon said, motioning Carlos into his office. "What's up?"

Carlos settled in the creaky chair across from Jon's desk. "I'm going to have to put in my two weeks," he explained.

Jon was shocked. "You're leaving?" he stammered. "Why? Where?"

"Nothing personal," Carlos lied. He had started looking for a new job months ago. He was tired of trying to keep his crew upbeat despite the constant pressure and negativity from Jon. "It was a surprise to me, but it's a position I can't turn down."

Jon tried to mask his disappointment as Carlos described his new position and what a good career move it would be for him. "OK, well, I'm happy for you, but it won't be the same around here without you," Jon said.

They shook hands, and Carlos left to join the crews in the break room for their morning meeting. Jon sat silently, running the situation through his mind. Carlos was one of his top guys. Who did he have to replace him? He wracked his brain trying to figure out who was ready to step up and take on more responsibility as a crew lead. *I have no one ready to replace Carlos*, he realized.

He shot off a text to Stu. "Just heard, Carlos put in notice to quit. What do I do?"

Stu's response came quickly, "Well, that stinks."

Um, yeah! Jon silently agreed.

Stu's more reasonable response followed quickly. "You'll need to figure out a plan to replace him. Check with Lisa in HR."

Jon nodded to himself and crafted a short email to Lisa, asking to meet with her to discuss recruiting for Carlos's position. It would take longer than two weeks to hire his replacement, so he would have to figure out a game plan in the interim. Jon felt betrayed by Carlos's decision, thinking, *He's planned this, just to make my life difficult.*

I wonder if I can put someone temporarily in his position, to see how they do? he wondered. "But who?" he asked out loud. Over the next two weeks, as Carlos worked out his notice, Jon acted out his feelings of betrayal and frustration over the situation. He was short with crew members and gave Carlos the silent treatment whenever he saw him. "I taught him everything he knows, and this is the thanks I get?" he fumed to his wife one evening. "Seriously, he didn't know anything when he first started. I took him under my wing and helped him every step of the way."

On his last day, the crews threw a going-away party for Carlos. Jon could no longer avoid Carlos, and he found himself in the back of the break room with him, silently sipping coffee and balancing plates of cake. Jon couldn't hold back any longer. "Thanks for putting me in a bind," his voice dripped with sarcasm.

"No problem," Carlos sparred back. But his tone turned more serious, "You know," he said softly, "there are plenty of guys on the crew who could easily replace me, if they were given an opportunity to learn and take on more responsibility."

Jon was not in the mood to be schooled by Carlos, but he nodded in agreement, then said, "Take care, buddy," as he quietly turned to leave. Alone again in his office, their exchange tumbled around in his head. *Was Carlos right? Could I have been investing more time in building up the crew?* It was true he didn't have a successor for Carlos, or any of the other leads.

I've been focused so much on what people aren't doing, or aren't doing right, that I haven't noticed anyone's potential.

He pulled out a sheet of paper, drew a line down the middle, and began to list his crew members, their strengths, and where he thought each could improve. He pored over the sheet, examining which crew members he could begin to give more responsibility (noted with an asterisk), who needed more training (identified by a capital "T"), and who might benefit from rotating to different functional areas. If he was going to have a crew capable of more responsibility, he would need to build up their knowledge and abilities. *And their confidence,* he acknowledged. Building up their confidence, skills, and commitment would be key for the future of Jon's crews. Before he left for the day, he scribbled out a schedule for the following day to visit each job site. *We'll see how it goes,* he told himself.

POTENTIAL INSTEAD OF PROBLEMS

At the previous Moving into Leadership session, the class spent time discussing the importance of recognizing and rewarding the positive contributions of team members.

"Look for examples of brilliance," the facilitator advised. "Always remember that people will continue to do what they're positively rewarded for. If you look for problems, you'll find them. But if you look for brilliance, you'll find that, too. Where are you placing your focus?"

Jon thought about the question, "Where do you place your focus?" and realized he rarely gave compliments. *Why am I so stingy with the thank-yous?* he wondered.

On the heels of Carlos leaving, Jon was making it a point to observe his crews in action and delegate more responsibility to them. He held true to his promise to allow crew leads to run the morning meetings without him, but continued, as usual, to be a regular fixture at job sites. If the crews were paying attention, however, they would have found Jon to be more detached and less involved than usual. Instead of hovering with a critical eye, Jon was doing his best to simply watch and observe, looking for what people were doing well. It was a difficult transition for him to make, shifting from involved participant to detached observer. He kept falling back into his old patterns of correcting and directing, but when he caught himself doing that, he would make as quick an exit as possible.

In his truck, he would jot down anything and everything he saw the crew doing that was correct, positive, helpful, considerate, or just plain good.

It took him several weeks of trying to retrain what he looked for while observing his crews, because his critical eye was always so engaged. But like strengthening an underused muscle, his eye for the positive began to develop. It wasn't that he wasn't still finding the problems, because he was! But it was becoming easier for him to spot what people were doing correctly. He noticed little things, like crew members bringing in special treats, helping each other out, and giving each other encouragement. There was a spirit of appreciation as high fives and thank-yous went around the room. He noticed crew members looking out for each other ("Don't forget your goggles") and signs of care and concern ("You OK there?"). The more he looked for examples of positive and helpful behavior, the more he found them. When left to perform on their own, his crews stepped up to the plate and committed themselves fully to the task at hand. They collaborated on problems and were clever and thrifty. A sense of pride swept over him.

Geez, he scolded himself. *When's the last time I gave them any positive news?*

YET ANOTHER MEETING

The crew didn't know what to think when Jon announced he was adding yet another weekly meeting to their schedule. Many wondered, *Now what? What is he going to berate us about now?* and *What have we done wrong this time?* The crews were apprehensive as they arrived that Friday morning and found Jon looking stern and serious in the front of the room. He allowed them time to help themselves to donuts and coffee, then called the group to order. "Let's go ahead and get started," he announced loudly, trying to get their attention.

"Good morning, everyone," he announced again, waiting until the group settled in. "Listen, we need to talk about a few things." His tone was somber. He took a deep breath. "First, I just want to say that Corey, Nancy, and Dillon," (the three looked back and forth at each other nervously, unsure as to why they were being called out in front of the entire group) "the way you used that sheeting to shore up the side of that ditch while you were fixing that break was sheer brilliance. How the heck did you come up with that? I never would've thought of that. Well done."

The three crew members relaxed a little and smiled big at the compliment.

"That fix was a little out-of-the-box, but it was safe, which I care about most, and it did was it was supposed to do, so it worked. That's the kind of ingenuity I like."

There were a few heckles from the room, all in good fun. "I taught him that!" Barry teased from the other side of the room.

"OK, OK," Jon said, using his hands to quiet the group down. He began again, with the same serious inflection. "On another matter, we also had some residents in an uproar over on Josephine Street on Tuesday. You know, I may not say it enough, but we need to always remember we're not just in the water business. We're in the customer service business. Bobby and Sam," he said, his stern look breaking into a smile, "kudos for being so professional with the residents on that street. I remember telling all of you that sometimes you have to just take time with people and answer their questions, especially from neighbors and residents. Sam and Bobby did that. I got word that several residents called in and said they were thankful you explained the timelines to them. You were excellent ambassadors of the division. Great work."

The two smiled, and more friendly heckling went around the room. For the next few minutes, Jon gave specific feedback to members of the other two crews, noting an example about safety gear and another one about a clean work site. He called out specific behaviors, ones that other crew members could easily replicate if they chose to. By the end of the short meeting, the entire team was laughing and cheering each other on.

"A final note: As soon as I know what direction we're taking with Carlos's replacement, I'll let you know. I'm still working with Stu on that. For now, you three," he pointed to Dillon, Sam, and Jay, "will stay on your temporary assignments. Any questions? OK, that's it for now. We've got a lot to get done today. Have a great day and a good weekend," Jon said. As the group began to disperse, he gave one last shout-out.

"One more thing: Work safe and work smart."

The energy was high as the crew members gathered in their respective teams. Jon felt like the morning—and his mission to recognize and acknowledge his team—was time well-spent. Feeling accomplished, he headed up to his office to grab his hard hat and once again observe his teams in action. He was beginning to enjoy his new focus on the positives. He felt happier and more productive than he had in a long time.

TEAM IT UP

Jon's crew members were getting used to the many different meetings Jon held:

- daily, morning "tailgate" meetings conducted by the crew leads for daily assignments
- monthly team meetings with Jon to review safety protocol and introduce any new policies
- weekly, Friday "pep" meetings where Jon acknowledges good work and shows his appreciation to the crews

Jon was noticing an annoying pattern in his meetings, however, and he wanted to figure out a solution. *Why is it I do most of the talking in these meetings?* he wondered one afternoon. He decided to explore ways to encourage his crew to participate more in his meetings. "My meetings," he said out loud in his office. *My meetings. That's the problem,* he realized. *I'm treating the meetings as mine instead of the teams'. Maybe it's time I handed some of the responsibility over to them.*

At the next Friday pep meeting, as they came to be called, Jon showed up and was eager to implement his idea. These Friday morning meetings had become one of the highlights of his week, when he showcased the talent and ingenuity on his team. He began the meeting as usual, offering examples of great work, innovation, and brilliance. Then he made his announcement. "In keeping with the theme of celebration and appreciation, I'm going to ask each of you to bring examples of positive performance to share at our next Friday meeting."

Jon ignored the good-natured ribbing from the group: "There is none!" and "When I see some, I'll let you know." Instead, he brought them back to attention. "I'm serious. I can only recognize the good things I see. But each of you are also out and about, working with each other, and you see much more than I. As a matter of fact, I know you all thank and congratulate each other on a daily basis. I'm asking you to each bring one example of something positive a coworker did so the rest of us are aware. It's all of our responsibility to be recognizing and celebrating the great work we all do."

His directive seemed to strike a chord with the team, and the group erupted in side conversations and laughter.

"OK, OK, so let's all be on the lookout for positives. That's all I have for today, so let's get out there and have a great day, and, what do we do?" The group was already dispersing, so he shouted out to them as they were leaving, "Work safe and work smart!"

Jon headed back to his office to prepare for his day. As a result of weekly meetings with his crew leaders, Jon was up to date on the progress of each crew, which allowed him to keep his eye on the bigger picture. He actually had time this afternoon to begin outlining his idea for a new training plan for junior crew members. He had several other items on his to-do list, including registering himself and the other crew leads for a regional training conference and reviewing a requisition for new equipment the team leads submitted to him.

Reflecting on his crew, he was noticing a real transformation occurring. The crews seemed more talkative, more cohesive, and happier. By implementing a few small measures, such as giving his team members more responsibility and focusing on the positives, Jon was building trust. For the first time in a while, Jon was beginning to feel as though he was leading four crews rather than doing the work of four crews.

BUILDING BRILLIANCE

When Avery and Jon accepted their leadership positions, they inherited a team of performers. They didn't have much opportunity to put together their own dream team. *It's a little like family,* Jon realized, *you get who you get!* His crews consisted of employees with varying levels of skill and motivation. While some crew members were novices, most were long-term employees who, like him, grew up at Axion and knew the organization and their jobs inside out.

Avery's team, too, consisted mostly of seasoned professionals. Each brought years of experience working at different companies before they joined Axion. Given such varied backgrounds, Avery was often surprised by the expertise and knowledge they possessed.

Avery and Jon would come to appreciate the special kind of magic that happens when the diversity within a team is honored. Recognizing and putting that talent to use is the first step in building a strong team.

Their teams were not only diverse in terms of skills, knowledge, and capabilities, but were diverse in terms of:

- age
- educational background
- race
- ethnicity
- gender
- sexual orientation
- physical ability
- work experience
- family status
- marital status
- hobbies and interests
- goals and ambitions

In addition, their teams also exhibited differences in terms of:

- personality styles
- reactions to conflict
- approaches to problem-solving
- communication styles
- learning styles
- comfort with technology

At first, Avery didn't realize the wealth of talent she had at her disposal. She knew some of her employees were more productive than others; in fact, she had a few rock stars on her team. Yet she didn't associate talent with output. She figured people did their jobs in whatever way they could.

"When your talents and interests align with the work you're doing, it doesn't seem like work at all. In fact, you get more done, quicker, more effectively, and with more creativity when you're working from your strengths," the facilitator had explained.

"Think back to the last time you lost track of time at work? What were you doing prior?" the facilitator had asked.

A recent experience immediately came to Avery's mind. She was creating process maps on her whiteboard in her office. She remembered the feeling of happiness and excitement as she scribbled ideas on the board, erased a few, and rewrote others, all in the quest for the perfect process outline. She stood back to admire her work from a distance, and, glancing at her clock, noticed that more than two hours had elapsed! She had failed to notice people leaving for the day, doors shutting, voices trailing off down the hallway. Lost in the energy of working through her strengths, time had simply slipped away.

At the same workshop, Jon, who typically didn't share personal reflections with the class, explained the last time he lost track of time. "I was with a crew, and we were studying an iPad, trying to align some locate data to the actual terrain. The three of us were working as a team, and it was a lot of fun. I didn't realize we had been talking for almost half an hour."

Avery thought about her team members and the work they did. Was she capitalizing on their strengths and talents? Was she allowing Lindsay to apply her people skills and Sandy to put her organizational abilities to use? Did she capitalize on Dennis's artistic ability and Dave's keen analytical brain? The more she began to slow down and watch and listen and observe her employees in action, the more she began to clearly see the talents they brought to their work.

The facilitator had made the point that great leaders don't try to change people but instead capitalize on their unique talents. Rather than try to fix or replace what's left out, they "try to help each person become a better version of themself"[11]

We all want to feel as though our skills, talents, and passions can be put to good use, but I don't know if I'm doing enough of this, Avery wondered. "How do you balance letting people use their strengths with also challenging them and helping them stretch beyond their comfort zone?" she asked the facilitator during that session.

"That's a great question, Avery," the facilitator replied. "Does anyone have any thoughts for Avery about how to balance these two seemingly different needs?"

Jon, too, was trying to figure out how to develop his crew members and capitalize on their strengths. Especially since losing several crew members, he realized a surefire way to keep his crew busy and productive was to challenge them and keep them learning new things.

"One thing I've learned," Jon shared, "is that each of my crew members approaches the same task in a slightly different way. At first, I wanted everyone to do things the right way, which was my way," he paused, hoping for a laugh from the class. Hearing none, he continued, "I have started giving them assignments and tasks and allowing them to schedule their own work. They seem to really like that. As long as they're not breaking any rules, are safe, and get it done on time, I'm good. I mean, I still want them to do it my way, but I decided that's not what's most important. I want my guys to be happy and feel good about their own work," he said.

"Sounds like a very good approach, Jon," the facilitator said, "because it really is important that our employees have a sense of accomplishment over the work they perform. What about some of the rest of you? How do you help your team members learn new things but also use their talents?"

Keith said, "I have one help desk staff member who is passionate about gaming. I mean, she lives for it. So I asked her if she would be willing to create a game to teach staff about Axion's policies on software security."

"That's so cool," Michelle said.

"Yeah," Keith continued, "it's almost completed, and it *is* very cool. She's got it set up so you are battling the forces of good and evil as a computer user. Each decision you make in the game creates either a positive or negative domino effect that affects Axion."

"I have an employee on my team," said Eddie from HR, "who is also very creative. Maybe she and your person can collaborate and create a game to explain the new processes for this year's open enrollment?"

Keith smiled and said, "That's a great idea."

"Now that I think about it," Avery interjected, "by pairing two of my employees [she was referring to Shannon and Brian] who each brings opposite strengths and talents, we could create this amazing dream team. I should talk with them and give them more team projects to capitalize on the natural synergy that occurs when Shannon's detail meets Brian's artistic talent."

"Now you're talking," the facilitator exclaimed. "Of course, there are times when we all must buck up and do work that's not our favorite, but when we can manage it, it's far more interesting and effective to put our true talents to work. I think you all are getting the idea."

Think about and assess the breadth of diversity on your team. How does this diversity positively contribute to your team? What are some ways you can harness that diversity and capitalize on it?

What impact do you believe Jon's shift—from seeking problems to seeking brilliance—will have on his team's morale and productivity?

Think back to an experience when you lost track of time. What sort of work or task were you doing, and why did it energize you? What would it be like if all your team members were using their strengths and talents to their full potential?

chapter 13

Risk-Taking and a
Focus on the Future

AVERY LOOKED FORWARD to the monthly Moving into Leadership sessions. In contrast to past workshops she attended, this one was different. It was giving her real skills and real insights to transform the way she led her team. And she was seeing results, too. Since she implemented regular meetings with her employees, Avery's team was more cohesive, productive, and ambitious than when she first came on board.

She was growing as a professional, too, through her interactions with colleagues in the program. Some of the insights they brought to the workshops were extremely valuable, and Avery found herself trying many of their ideas. For example, during a recent session, Keith shared that his team members each take a turn in facilitating the team meetings.

"And they do it?" Avery asked.

"Oh yeah," Keith replied. "I started with some of the more outgoing employees, for whom it wasn't so much of a stretch. But this way, it forces everyone to pay attention and take responsibility for what we discuss. And it gives me the chance to participate as a member of the team rather than always facilitating."

Avery was interested in this approach. Although she was a stickler about her one-on-one meetings, she was known for canceling her team meetings. *They were so dry and boring! No one really gets anything out of them,* she believed.

But she learned that Jon, too, was investing time and attention in his team meetings. "We all share kudos with each other at our Friday meeting," Jon explained, with a hint of pride in his voice. "So far, it's creating a lot of positive energy."

Avery thought long and hard about the idea of incorporating structure into her team meetings. She didn't want to turn people off with this, but there had to be a way to make team meetings more productive and interesting. She was lost in her thoughts about Jon's and Keith's ideas when she was interrupted by a soft rap on her door.

"Come in," she said, before turning to see Dave at her door. "Hey there, come on in."

Dave entered and sat in the chair across from her. He fidgeted in his seat.

"What can I do for you?"

"Darla has completed her nursing program and is now being accepted into rotation at Meyer's General," he began.

"Well, that's exciting," Avery replied, turning to focus her attention on Dave. "Tell her I said congratulations."

"I will," he said. "It's, uh, well, it's created a few complications that we weren't expecting, though," he continued.

Avery pushed her chair slightly away from her desk, signaling for him to continue. "Unfortunately, she's been put on days, which is great for her, but it means we'll both be working the same shift," he explained.

The complications for Dave and Darla began to unfold for Avery. Their youngest daughter, Christy, required specialized care. Darla's new shift would create scheduling issues for them both. Because of Christy's condition, day care or nannies weren't a feasible option for the family.

"We're trying to figure out a solution, but there's no way both of us can work the same shift and take care of Christy." He paused and took a deep breath, then asked, "I was wondering if we could discuss some work-from-home options for me?"

Since Avery and Dave had begun meeting regularly and working together, Dave had become one of Avery's most trusted employees and she was fast-tracking him, among others on her team, for internal promotion. By no means did she want to lose this bright and ambitious employee, but she wasn't sure if or how she could accommodate his request.

She pursed her lips and was silent for a few moments, trying to figure out how to deliver the bad news. Telecommuting was largely discouraged by the organization, and Axion's vague work-from-home policy didn't offer much guidance. Avery, herself, wasn't much of a fan of working from home. It seemed frivolous and lazy. *What percentage*, she often wondered, *of those who work from home actually work?* "Probably not many," she remembered complaining to her wife one weekend after watching a news show highlighting the increase in telecommuting and how it was slowly changing the workplace in many industries. She felt it was an either-or proposition: either be self-employed and work from home, or have a real job and work at an office. Her balance-sheet personality style led her to believe never the two should meet, so her instinct was to explain why she couldn't accommodate his request. It wasn't solely security concerns, or the lack of budget for the necessary technology; the concern was for equity and how it would be perceived as favoritism to allow Dave such a privilege. If she allowed Dave to work from home, she'd have to accommodate everyone, and that could potentially be a logistical nightmare for the department.

I just don't have the resources or the patience to be trendy, she thought.

"I'm going to have to think about it, Dave," she answered.

"Sure, sure," he replied, getting up to leave, "I totally understand."

She mulled over the circumstances. *On the one hand, Dave has become one of my most reliable employees. I can't afford to lose him. Do I want to risk losing such a high performer because he's requesting change?*

On the other hand, she thought, *what do I gain if I allow him to work from home? Could there be benefits that I'm not yet seeing? As a leader, am I supposed to maintain the status quo? Or find opportunities for change?*

Her thoughts turned to a cost-benefit analysis of losing Dave versus transitioning the department into a virtual unit. She sketched out a decision tree on her whiteboard, scribbling costs and projections along with gains and benefits as she went. Later that afternoon, she sent a text to Dave:

"Dave, come by my office when you get a chance."

Within minutes, Dave was back at her door. She waved him in.

"OK, here's where I'm at. Your predicament is tricky. I want to be able to accommodate you, because you're an asset to my team, but I also have to consider the needs of the team. But I was thinking maybe your situation is an opportunity—an opportunity to expand how we do business, hopefully for the better. Maybe it's time we dipped a toe into the virtual landscape."

Her response not only surprised Dave; it surprised her, too, as she said it out loud. Without even noticing, Avery made one of her first, true leadership decisions—a decision that was premised on the future needs of her team and future benefits for the organization. This was, for her, the first time she was making a decision that had implications not only for her, but for her team. It felt like a different level of decision—one at a level she wasn't used to making. And she would have to make a strong case to Ken about its benefits in order to move forward. In that moment, her decision felt right.

"When does Darla start her new shift?" she asked.

"We have some flexibility, but technically her new rotation begins next month," he replied.

"OK. I'm going to need you to think through as many logistics as you can and put a proposal together outlining how you see this working," Avery instructed, "and as soon as possible. I would say get me a rough, rough draft by end of week. Let's get moving on this sooner rather than later."

"Will do," he agreed. "I haven't thoroughly worked it all out, but was hoping I could work from home three days a week, then be in office for two, with the flexibility to rotate those days based on the circumstances of my wife's schedule."

"This is your deal," she explained. "But we're not implementing telecommuting solely for you; we're implementing it departmentwide, so make sure your proposal doesn't just meet your personal needs but will work for as many on the team as possible."

"Got it," he said.

"Once you have your ideas together, I'm going to ask Brian to head this up. We'll bring in others on the team, too, as a planning committee," she explained.

"Got it," he repeated. Dave wiped a small tear from the corner of his eye as he rose to exit her office. "Thanks," he mouthed.

She nodded and smiled. "No problem."

STEPPING INTO THE FUTURE

"There are times when I'd like to participate in our discussions as a participant and less as the leader," Avery said at the next team meeting. "I'm wondering if others of you would be willing to occasionally step up to run the meetings?"

Several team members, including Sandy and Dennis, spoke up, volunteering.

"Thank you," Avery said, acknowledging the volunteers. "I'll work with each of you to formulate an agenda. But it will be up to you to determine the format and the process," she said. "If this goes well, I would expect us to routinely rotate as facilitators. Who knows? Our meetings could become slightly less boring." She paused, looking for reactions. "They should be *our* meetings, not just mine."

The team meeting was already abuzz after Avery announced this new format change. In their typical teasing fashion, the team wailed out loud as a form of protest. But despite their protesting, most of them appreciated Avery's continued focus on the team. "These are not just *my* meetings," Avery repeated.

"Could've fooled me," teased Alice.

Feeling as though the group was primed to take on even more change, she cautiously launched into her next agenda item.

"Finally," she said, her tone shifting to a more serious one, "I believe there will come a time when we'll need to be comfortable delivering services while remote." Sensing the confusion in the room, Avery continued, explaining that Dave would be piloting a work-from-home program.

Dave interjected, explaining, "My wife has begun her internship rotation, but that means we'll both be working the same shift. I asked Avery if there was any way I could work a few days from home," he paused, trying to gauge his teammates' reactions. "You know, so one of us would be there for Christy." His voice trailed off.

Avery continued. "While I realize this is a shift in how we typically work, I think it will bring a lot of benefits to us and how we deliver services."

Alice interrupted, "You mean we all might be able to occasionally work from home?"

"Yes. Not only able to," Avery clarified, "but expected to." She paused, waiting for her statement to sink in with the group. Avery hoped the rest of the team would be excited by the possibility of bringing more balance to their lives. While she hadn't run the idea past Ken yet, she had come to believe it was the right and current course of action.

"I don't see how that would work," Shannon said.

"There are a lot of questions and details that will need to be addressed—make no mistake about it. And we'll need to demonstrate the business case for implementing this policy. Our health and wellness as employees are important, but we also need to show that we can be just as effective—no, more effective—if we have remote capabilities. There are likely benefits and possibilities that we can't even imagine yet. That's why I'd like to create a team to research costs, identify benefits, review potential barriers, and make recommendations," Avery said.

The team began to talk openly, sharing ideas and concerns. Avery brought them back to order. "I've asked Dave to do some preliminary research on industry best practices," she said, "but we'll need more input." Avery raised her voice to be heard over the din. "I want one representative from each functional area to work with Dave to research and create recommendations for our policy," she said, lowering her voice.

"Please let Dave know if you're interested in contributing your ideas to this project. This is about us making ourselves relevant and current. Be thinking about how you would be able to manage your workload if you were working from home," she said. "We will be fore-runners in the organization, and, I suspect, probably in the industry." The team continued to talk after she adjourned the meeting.

"Brian, do you have a few minutes for me?" she asked. They headed back to her office together.

PASSING TORCHES

"The prospect of creating bandwidth for our team to work virtually is extremely exciting to me," Avery said, speaking as she moved across the room to her chair. "And I would ask you to oversee this project."

"What do you mean?" he asked.

"Well, Dave and others will begin researching, but I'd like you to lead their project team," she explained. "Review their research, and work with them to evaluate their findings, and prepare a set of recom-mendations and a proposal, which I'll then use to pitch to Ken and the rest of the senior team."

"Oh, OK, sure," he said, with a bit of hesitation, "but I don't really know where to begin."

"I'll work with you to get you started, but you've done this sort of project before. It's no different from analyzing usage and making recommendations on rate increases. The difference is the research affects us internally instead of an external audience," she explained. "This is a great opportunity for us," she corrected herself, "for you, to highlight your leadership skills."

"Well, thanks," Brian responded, seeming a bit surprised, "I appreciate it."

"Just pretend that you came up with the idea, and run with it," she teased, giving him a smile. "Listen to what the project team proposes, and help the team think through the data. I'll want your draft recommendations by our next scheduled one-on-one. Dave will need to begin to work from home within two weeks, so that will be a great, practical way to test the water. We can use his experiences to learn as we go."

They chatted for a while longer, with Brian verbalizing a potential game plan and Avery asking him questions, until she finally shooed him off. Sitting in the temporary quiet of her office, she reflected on her decision. She was authorizing what would be construed as an extremely controversial initiative for Axion. Previously, she would have jumped into high gear, researching, and figuring out *can we do this telecommuting thing?* on her own. But this time she delegated responsibility to her team and transferred authority to Brian. She would then evaluate their research and assess their recommendations, which was truly a different role for her.

She turned to her PC and began to scroll through her emails, landing on a spreadsheet Alice had sent. "Do you really need to review that spreadsheet?" the voice of the facilitator from the leadership program echoed in her ear. She forwarded the spreadsheet back to Alice, asking her to "Please review for accuracy and then correct any errors. I'll need this back from you at least two days prior to our scheduled meeting. Thank you!"

She smiled to herself as she continued scanning emails, identifying a few that other members of her team could address instead of her. An email from HR regarding changes in personnel action forms caught her eye. She hit "forward" and began her message to Lindsay: "Lindsay," her email began, "you have worked most closely with HR on this one. Would you please be the point person on this? Let's plan to discuss at your next one-on-one on Monday. Thank you!"

The old Avery would worry that she was dumping work on her employees, but instead, Avery felt like she was doing the responsible thing by assigning the right talent to different tasks. She had an incredibly competent team of professionals who could and should be working independently and producing complex results. If she had anything to say about it, they would be.

for your consideration

Do you agree or disagree with Avery's decision to allow Dave to work from home? Why or why not?

What transformations are you noticing in Avery and her leadership style? What do you attribute these changes to?

What are you noticing about the intersection of trust, delegation, and communication as illustrated in this chapter?

chapter 14

Coach—and Get Out of Their Way

LISA RAN INTO AVERY in the administration building. "How are your meetings with staff going, Avery?" she asked.

Avery grinned. "You would think I was asking them to climb Mount Everest!" she explained. "They grumbled and complained for the first few months," she continued, "but you know what? I think everyone has really come to appreciate them. They've come to understand I'm not just there for them when there's a problem, but I'm there for them all the time."

Lisa smiled. "I'm hearing a lot of amazing feedback from your team members. Actually, I'm hearing positive things from employees from other teams. Whatever you're doing, it seems to be making a difference."

"Thanks," Avery responded. She was proud of the transition she'd made, from a stereotype of a boss to a genuine catalys:[12] someone who energizes her team and keeps them focused on achieving bigger and greater accomplishments. She challenges them and trusts them to make decisions and solve problems independently. Instead of just going through the motions, the individuals on her team are excelling. Meetings are energetic; there's a lightness in the office; information flows freely; and people smile much, much more. Even though she always liked her work at Axion, for the first time in a while she looked forward to coming in to work. She liked to think her team was happier, too.

"I wish more supervisors would take my advice," Lisa confided.

"I'm happy to be a walking testimonial for one-on-one meetings," Avery offered. She recalled her earlier skepticism about regular meetings with her employees, thinking there would be little to discuss or the meetings would feel trite. But once she started to meet regularly with her team members, everything changed. Her regular meetings allowed Avery to keep tabs on what was getting accomplished in her department, and everyone was compelled to stay focused and productive.

This changed her role. While she used to think it was her responsibility to correct her team members' mistakes, now team members catch their own mistakes, or bring problems to their meetings to solve together.

"The best thing I learned from the leadership program," she admitted to Lisa, "was how to ask better questions. This wasn't instinctual for me. I had to learn how to do this."

For example, if time isn't an issue, Avery is more likely to quiz her staff ("Isn't there a guideline around this? Would you research that and let me know?") rather than simply telling them what to do. She wants her employees to be smarter than she is, able to figure things out on their own.

"I'm sure they're all complaining to you about how I ask them, 'What are your recommendations?' or 'Tell me how we got to this point.' I think, if you ask my staff, they'll now tell you 'There are no easy answers with Avery.'"

"Sounds like you, and the team, have gone through quite the transformation," Lisa said.

"I know I certainly have," Avery admitted. "In fact, I've learned that their work is their work. It's their project. Or their customer. The hardest lesson I've learned is to get out of people's way."

She didn't share this with Lisa, but it was a real eye-opener for Avery when Dennis told her, during one of their early one-on-one meetings, "We don't need you to *do* our work; we just need your permission to perform, and perform in our own way."

Avery was holding them up, not helping them out! She would forever be grateful for Dennis's feedback and explanation on how she was hindering rather than helping. She recalled when Dennis told her, in no uncertain terms, "There are some things we need your direction on. And there are some decisions that only you can make. But the rest of the time, we should become experts in our jobs. The best help you can give us is to give us what we need to do our jobs."

"And sometimes," he went on, "we just need you to listen."

Avery remembered how significant that honest discussion was with Dennis. In fact, looking back, she was struck by how informative all the early one-on-one conversations were with her staff. They opened up, shared honestly, and gave her genuine feedback. When the facilitator referred to helpful feedback as "a gift," Avery knew precisely what she meant. Because of that feedback, Avery realized she didn't just show up every day to do a job; she was showing up to help many people do their jobs. It transformed how she viewed her role. And this transformation began to pay off in her relationships with her team.

For example, while Lindsay once viewed Avery as meddling in her work, she now better understands that Avery is genuinely interested in her success. The real shift for Lindsay happened when she stopped into Avery's office one afternoon.

"Hey, boss, quick question?" Lindsay said.

"You bet, Lindsay. What's up?"

"I got your email about the personnel action forms and the revised codes and, as we thought, we have some duplicate coding that will cause us problems down the road …" Lindsay paused, waiting for Avery's response.

"Hmmm. Well, what do you think is best to do?"

It took a moment for Avery's confidence in her to register before Lindsay responded, "Well, as you know, I've met with HR twice and IT once about this matter, and I thought everyone was on the same page. Turns out, HR is still confused. I guess I can set up a meeting with just Sue and me and walk her through which departments have duplicate codes. That way, I can address any questions and possibly even clear up discrepancies. I know we're on a tight deadline for implementation."

"That sounds reasonable to me," Avery replied. "And that's probably what I would do, too. Plan to update me at our next one-on-one unless you run into a significant snag."

"Sounds good!" Lindsay was gone before Avery could say another word.

Avery thought back to when she first started at Axion and took on the catering faux pas from Dennis. In hindsight, it was a problem that

Dennis easily could have handled on his own. *Why did I think I needed to handle that catering issue for him or the scheduling issue for Sandy?* she wondered. *I've come a long way,* she smiled to herself.

for your consideration

In what way do you think Avery's perception of leadership has changed?

If you were coaching Avery, what behaviors or practices would you encourage her to continue? And which would you encourage her to change or modify?

Identify some examples of effective coaching that Avery exhibits in this chapter.

What are you noticing about the intersection of trust, delegation, and communication as illustrated in this chapter?

chapter 15

PROFESSIONAL DEVELOPMENT: SPEAKING OF PERFORMANCE REVIEWS...

"LISTEN, YOU'RE NOT THE ONLY ONE WHO can delegate," Ken said.

"Oh, no, I'm not a public speaker" Avery said.

"I'm not asking you to become a professional speaker," Ken persisted, "but I think it would be a good experience for you. And besides, I think you'll bring a lot to the topic."

Ken had been asked to speak at the annual finance officers conference but couldn't attend because the date conflicted with his twenty-fifth anniversary trip to Maui. He offered Avery as a competent substitute. "It'll be in Vegas," he said, hoping to sweeten the deal. He pantomimed pulling the handle of a slot machine.

"And besides, you'll be part of a panel, so it's not as if you'll be up on a stage by yourself."

Avery shuddered at the idea of speaking to an audience in any capacity, whether by herself or as a member of a panel. *So this is what it feels like to be outside of your comfort zone*, she thought. She reflected back to a conversation months earlier with Shannon.

"But I'm not good at pivot tables," Shannon had protested.

"You don't need to be an expert at them," Avery told her, "but it's always good to challenge yourself and learn something new. It may feel uncomfortable now, but over time I think you'll master them. And besides, the team really could use another expert in pivot tables."

How easy it was to challenge Shannon, but when it came to challenging herself, it wasn't so easy.

"You've been doing so many great things with your team," Ken continued. "I think you'll bring a lot of great ideas as a panelist."

"What's the topic?" Avery asked.

"Performance reviews," he replied. "Right up your alley."

Avery cradled her head in her hand, shaking her head from side to side. "I can't believe in any way that this will be a good idea," she said.

The actual title of the panel was "Performance Reviews: Outdated Rhetoric or Essential Practice?" Avery took every opportunity to prepare for her role as a panelist. She wrote her remarks, and even wrote answers to potential questions she might be asked by audience members. Even though she rehearsed her responses over and over again, she still felt sick to her stomach from nerves. She was nervous and anxious leading up to the actual conference and nauseated on the morning of the panel. She felt out of sorts and awkward. *What if I blank up there?* she worried.

She took her seat at the long table at the front of the conference room. There were probably twenty audience members already seated throughout the room. More people filled the room. The moderator introduced each panelist, then posed the first question.

"So many of us have become frustrated with performance reviews," the moderator began. "Is it time to reconsider their value? Should we abandon them, or are they still an essential element in today's workplace?"

It was interesting to hear the different perspectives of the panelists. Avery was the third to speak. She began, hesitantly at first, but as she started speaking, her nerves subsided. "I would say I'm an advocate for keeping performance reviews. I've implemented a number of practices that have helped transform how we feel about them." She paused, scanning her notes, then began again.

"I conduct regular one-on-one meetings with each of my employees," she explained, "and have a dedicated hour for each of them. It's really been an effective practice, I think, because my employees know they have my undivided attention, so it's reduced any level of competition they have toward each other." She explained that competition had been partly behind a rift between two of her staff members. But since she implemented one-on-ones, she's seen very little tension or competition among staff members.

"These monthly meetings allow me to acknowledge the work that each team member is doing. I try to give them constructive feedback whenever possible. And then all the notes I keep from these meetings," she held up one of the spiral notebooks she brought from the office, "become the data for their annual performance reviews."

The previous panelist had shared that she dreaded performance reviews and found them a waste of time.

"I used to think they were bogus, too," Avery admitted, looking her way, "but now I think they're a great opportunity to celebrate my staff. The first few performance reviews I conducted weren't helpful, because I didn't have any documentation or data for them. I typically just wrote something like, 'Great job, Shannon. Keep up the good work! Shannon is a valuable member of my team.'

"It must not have been very satisfying to receive such vague feedback after working for an entire year for me!" she confessed. "But when you think about it, weak feedback, or ineffective feedback on a performance evaluation, is probably a big part of the reason why we're questioning the value of them today. I mean, generic feedback doesn't help employees understand what they're doing correctly, and it certainly doesn't help them correct deficiencies or improve. How can employees know if they're frustrating you, or missing the mark, if you don't let them know? How can employees rectify problems if they're not informed about them? Lacking any input, employees are simply left on their own to manage their own behavior, and in my experience, that's a big problem.

"I think it's my obligation to keep ongoing records of what my employees accomplish, which then helps me justify pay increases or promotions, or substantiate requests for training or conferences, like these." Avery was beginning to capture the attention of the data-driven accountants in the room.

"How do you make time for that?" came a voice from the audience.

Avery had almost forgotten she was speaking in front of a group, and the question from the audience jolted her back. She paused, waiting to see if another panelist would respond. Hearing nothing, she continued.

"I thought I wouldn't have time to both meet with my employees *and* keep good documentation," she said, "but actually? It was more work when I was writing notes in retrospect, you know, when I had to try to remember something someone did, or remember the details of a special project that happened. That was the time-consuming part. But now that I keep ongoing notes, it hardly takes much time at all.

"I have a notebook for each employee," she continued, holding up the prop she brought. "I know it's a little old-school, but there's something about it that works for me. I take written notes during my one-on-ones, which my staff members watch me do, and then I later transcribe relevant notes into our online performance management portal," she explained.

The moderator posed a new question to the panel: "It's one thing for us, as leaders, to understand the benefits of performance evaluations, but how do we get employees to take the process seriously?"

When it was Avery's turn to speak, she explained that she used to worry that her employees would think she was checking up on them. As she told it, "Would they think I'm checking up on them or trying to get them in trouble? Would they be fearful I would use my notes against them? But once my staff started to realize that my notes weren't a secret, and that I use these notes to help them, it changed everything. We openly talk about pretty much everything in our regular one-on-one meetings, and I share the notes I make about their performance. It's all out in the open. So maybe the transparency of my process reduces any anxiety they may feel. They also know that I maintain records of any problems and how problems were fixed."

Another panelist shared, "Our employees also contribute to their documentation. I can't be everywhere and know everything that employees are accomplishing. Because our system is electronic, employees can add notes and see my notes in real time."

At this, Avery also interjected, "We also have an electronic system that allows everyone to communicate and add notes. At some point, I'll probably ditch the paper notebooks and just take notes electronically. I'm just not there yet. I like the ritual of filing away the paper notebook and bringing out a brand-new one at everyone's end-of-year evaluation meeting."

"Thank you, everyone," the moderator said. "We have time to take questions from the audience …"

"I just wanted to add," Avery interrupted. "I just wanted to add, in response to the last question about how we get employees to take performance evaluations seriously, in my meetings with my staff and through our evaluation process, we have a give-and-take with feedback. I make it a point to learn my employees' goals so I can target my feedback to help them. I take their goals seriously. And any feedback I give them, whether it's positive or constructive, is to help them advance in their careers and achieve their goals. I think my employees are starting to realize that I'm here to help them succeed, and that's made all the difference."

The rest of the session was a back-and-forth between the audience and the panelists. Avery found herself almost eager to answer questions from the audience and share her techniques for documentation, feedback, and meetings.

"I also ask my employees to come prepared with feedback on my performance," Avery said. "It's a little scary and a little risky," she admitted, "but feedback should go both ways. I want to help my employees grow, and I want to develop as a leader. So, I need their input just as they need mine."

"What feedback have you received from your employees?" an audience member asked.

"Well, one employee told me that I don't give them enough instruction and direction. Another told me that they like how I ask for their recommendations and opinions on matters. There is usually no shortage of feedback from my staff about how I'm doing." The audience laughed with her.

Before she knew it, the session was over.

"Let's give a round of applause to all of our panelists today," the moderator said, concluding the session.

"Great job," one audience member told her after the session ended.

"Thanks," Avery said, finally feeling a sense of relief. "I was so nervous," she admitted.

"Really? You couldn't tell," came the reply.

I guess that wasn't as bad as I thought, she told herself, *although I don't think I'm going to quit my day job.*

for your consideration

What connections are you seeing between documentation, feedback, and employee development? Identify some examples from this chapter (or previous ones) that demonstrate how these three practices are integral to employee success.

In what ways do you think the experience of public speaking impacted Avery? What lessons can you take from this chapter about professional growth and development?

Professional (or personal) growth is often linked to experiences outside our comfort zones. Think back to a time when you stepped outside your comfort zone: What was the experience like? In what ways did you learn, discover, or benefit?

What role do leaders play in assisting in the growth and development of others?

chapter 16

FINDING PURPOSE
AS A LEADER

JON'S DAYS HAD A VASTLY DIFFERENT FEEL to them now. He still spent a lot of time out in the field, but his purpose was different.

"Jon!" crew members shouted, as he recently approached a job site.

"What'cha got going on today?" he asked, strolling over to them. Beaming, the crew members began to explain the situation and their plans. In the past, the crews would hold back and wait for Jon to tell them what to do or ask Jon, "Is that OK?" Jon used to be the butt of their jokes after work, as in "Oh yeah, the big guy always thinks he knows so much!" But Jon now hears none of that.

"You tell me," he's known to say, when a crew member appears to wait for his directive. "You're the expert! What do you think is best here?" Jon listens intently to the employee's explanation, interjecting an, "Uh-huh, interesting," or an occasional question such as, "What about installing a blow-off there?"

This profound shift occurred almost by accident. It was late one afternoon, and Jon watched one of the crews struggle to close a valve on a water pipe. Without realizing it, Jon had taken over while his crew—Dillon, Doug, and Sam—supervised him. Sweat was falling from his brow, and his jeans were wet and dirty.

"How's it going, boss?" Dillon asked in a cheery voice.

As if a light bulb went off, Jon realized he was more of a hindrance than a help. It embarrassed him to admit it, but working side by side with the crew was his way of demonstrating his worth. That afternoon, he discovered they didn't need his labor. They needed his leadership. Jon reached up and handed Sam the wrench, whispering under his breath, *Why am I doing this?*

Then, turning to the crew, he asked, "You guys got this?"

Dillon, who was closest, helped Jon out of the hole and said, "Yup. We got it, boss."

Since that last time in the ditch, Jon's changed his tune. Now, he tries to support and motivate his crews instead of doing the work for them. He wants to make sure his crews can assess a complex problem and then solve it on their own. His goal is to make sure his team members have considered all contingencies and are confident in how to proceed. He's learned if he tells them what to do, they're simply doers, not thinkers, and Jon realizes if he has critical thinkers who make sound choices, his teams get more done. He no longer spoon-feeds answers to his crew but instead coaches them until they figure out the answers on their own.

He's implemented his training program, which includes rotating crew members to different functional areas. Whenever possible, Jon tries to make each visit to a job site an educational moment for the entire crew, with the junior crew members gaining insight into process and techniques, while senior crew members analyze, assess, and share their expertise. He's been known to ask the most junior team member how to solve a problem. The first time he did so, the rest of the crew looked on anxiously, wondering, "What is his game? Is he trying to humiliate this young guy?" That new crew member hemmed and hawed until he tentatively offered an answer, to which Jon said, "Well, you are partially right. I like how you can think on your feet." The crew watched, in amazement, as Jon turned to Dillon, more senior, and asked the same question. Dillon perked up, offering his recommendation. "I think you've got it," Jon replied. "How did you come up with that?" Then he turned to Sam, who replaced Carlos, and asked, "And how do we verify that we have the correct valve?"

"Exactly," Jon replied as Sam demonstrated. He now encourages all crew members to work together to solve problems. Jon offers his approval, "Yup, that's what I would do. Good work." Or he coaches them through an issue. "Walk me through that," and "How'd you come up with that?"

Before he leaves any job site, he reminds them, "Work safe and work smart." One afternoon, the group surprised him by chiming in. Jon smiled with the satisfaction that his teams were becoming independent and competent.

Once a hawk, overseeing his crews, looking for mistakes or problems, Jon had become an eagle, soaring above, available to help when needed. He observes their progress to coordinate the work of other teams. Trusting his crews on the ground gives Jon the freedom to make more strategic decisions about allocating staff, resources, and equipment. In his meetings with the crews, he gains intelligence and information. His crew leads, in turn, have come to understand the level of information Jon needs from them and, therefore, give him more useful status updates. The progress reports and status updates he receives from his crew leads allow him to advocate for additional resources or time.

He and his crews have become partners, working together to assess needs, address challenges, and solve problems.

As a result of Jon's shift in how he manages his team, his crews have become more productive than ever. In fact, Jon's crews are the most requested internal transfers at Axion. Some of his team members, under his coaching, were promoted to other units across the organization. Emile accepted a promotion at another utility. For the first time in a long time, Jon has been really enjoying his job. The people side of things, that part that he used to dismiss, was now his favorite part about his role. He enjoys meeting with each crew member and helping them develop their own knowledge and skill so they can be productive. While he was once disappointed and bitter at the prospect of losing Carlos, Jon now considers it his responsibility to help his employees get promoted and earn more money and status. "That's my job," he explained to one of his newer crew members, Aaron. "I want you to be the best you can be, so you can one day take my job."

On the rare occasions when there has been an emergency, instead of barking out orders, Jon quietly observes, asks for input, and makes quick decisions if necessary. But he views his crew members as the experts on his team. He takes in information and then puts the right people on the task. No more jumping in the ditch to show off his expertise and handle the situation like a superhero! Jon's division is known across the organization as that division where people work and learn together.

At his standing meeting with his own boss, Stu, he was surprised to find him looking serious.

"There are a few things we need to discuss today, Jon," Stu said sternly. Jon was surprised by his tone and felt concerned.

"Apparently," Stu said, "others in the organization have been watching what's happening on your crews. So much so," as he spoke, his tone and body began to soften, and a big grin came on his face, "so much so that I'd like to offer you a promotion."

Jon was taken aback. "Promotion?" he asked.

"That's right," Stu said. "Whatever you've been doing to speed up response times has caught Marty's eye. In the midst of some reorganization, I've been asked to move to Plant Operations, and I'm here to ask you to step into my position on an acting basis. It would mean managing all five divisions under maintenance." Stu paused, then continued, "You will automatically be considered a candidate for the position when HR formally opens up the recruitment."

"It would mean a lot more responsibility, but we all believe that you're up for the job," Stu said.

"Why don't you take a few days and mull it over?" Stu suggested. "But I'll need to know your decision by close-of-business on Friday."

Jon said he would take the time to think it over, but he knew he would accept the position. He was eager for more responsibility and the possibility to apply the skills he learned over the past two years. He was already planning how he would handle that very first day in his new role.

Thinking back, Jon realized that Stu had used the same approach with him as Jon now used with his crew members. Stu guided Jon but didn't direct him; Stu encouraged him and celebrated the strengths and passions that Jon brought to the job. Stu helped Jon become a better version of himself, as true leaders do.

A LEAP OF FAITH

"I'm going to go ahead and approve your pilot," Ken told her.

"Thank you," Avery said. "I think we'll save money in the long run." It wasn't a hard sell to Ken. In the end, Ken and Avery both agreed that if her work-from-home pilot failed, they would learn valuable lessons. But if it was successful, they might increase productivity by giving employees more flexible work options. They might defray some costs, especially around leave, and would earn loyalty among employees, like Alice, who endured a long and stressful commute, or Sandy, who juggled work and school with caregiving responsibilities.

Avery left the meeting with Ken energized. She successfully pitched and sold a novel idea that not only benefitted her team but that could benefit the entire organization. An overwhelming sense of satisfaction and pride washed over her.

That week, Dave began working from home. He would work virtually every day except for Wednesdays. He and Avery scheduled two one-hour check-in meetings, one on Monday and one on Thursday. Since their team meetings were usually held on Tuesday mornings, he would attend using a video call-in.

The IT Department worked with Dave and Brian to secure licenses for Dave's home-based access to Wynsome, and it was easy to set up virtual access to the server. Working with IT, they checked and double-checked network connectivity from Dave's home and installed security software that updated weekly and ran sweeps on his hardware.

Since Dave would be in the office only on Wednesdays, which could change, he joked to the team, "Don't kick me out completely yet." Sandy would be sharing his office space, which would give her a more formal sense of place on the team. Previously, she just used a portion of the copy area for her work space. This way, she could have an office to, almost, call her own.

There was interest among others on the team to change their schedules and implement a virtual work schedule. Avery asked them to wait a month until she could evaluate how she felt things were going. "Let's please start slowly; then we can re-evaluate as we go," she said. While she was anxious to see results of their trial, even she was nervous they were doing too much, too soon. She told the group they would evaluate Dave's productivity and then slowly implement revised schedules for the rest of the team.

"As the committee recommended," she reminded the group, "we'll most likely implement one work-from-home day a week per person, with the option to increase to three days a week."

As a result of their experiment with virtual work, her department eliminated several redundancies in their work procedures.

"We're going to need very clear protocol as to how to handle approval of time cards if we—and supervisors and managers—are not in the office," Alice stated to the team. "I thought maybe we could put together a flowchart to help us stay consistent."

The billing clerks also created a script and a flowchart when answering citizen questions. The script eliminated the need for them to seek approval when creating payment plans for customers and eventually led to reduced customer callbacks. When they worked in the office together, they had inconsistent responses to customer problems, which often resulted in complaints. But now, they were a unified voice, even though they worked from different locations. The billing team was proud of how they were improving customer service with their new flowchart and script.

Ken and Avery had developed a comfortable partnership. During a regular check-in meeting, Ken told her, "I thought you did a great job presenting to the board."

"Thanks," she replied. "I'm getting a little more comfortable each time I give a presentation to the board. I think that experience speaking as a panelist at the conference helped."

"You fought me over that one," Ken said.

"I know," she replied.

Ken's tone shifted, "The board was very impressed with your work-from-home pilot program. You're not going to up and leave on me after all this, are you?"

Avery stammered, "Up and leave? What do you mean?"

"Well, now that you've been recognized by the board of directors for exceptional service to the organization …" he said, enjoying the air of mystery he had created.

"What are you talking about?" she asked, perplexed.

"Just what I said. The board is recognizing you for exceptional service." He pulled a large, white envelope from the top drawer of his desk and passed it over to her.

Avery smiled as she opened the envelope.

"For the work-from-home program you implemented," he explained.

"It wasn't me," she corrected. "It was purely a team effort. I just supported them. My team deserves all the credit. In fact, my team always seems to step up and make me look good."

for your consideration

What are some key lessons from this story that will positively impact the way you support your team?

chapter 17

Conclusion: The Artistry of Leadership

IT'S BEEN AN AMAZING JOURNEY FOR JON in his first few years as a leader. As he discovered, leadership isn't about being smarter or better than his team, and it's not about power, authority, or control. Instead, leadership is about building relationships, guiding others, and helping them achieve their highest potential. Jon came to understand that the people stuff is what makes leadership both rewarding *and* challenging. He learned that his team relied on him to create an environment that allowed them to flourish.

Once Jon began to view his role differently—as a coach and guide rather than a disciplinarian and expert—his relationships to his crew members changed, and so did the performance of his team. Once they believed he trusted and respected their abilities, his crew members went above and beyond his expectations. Feeling supported does that for people.

Avery's team has experienced its fair share of ups and downs. Sometimes leadership means making difficult decisions or addressing problems within the team. If you shy away from holding people accountable, or allow people to behave badly on the team, your employees may question your motives. After all, if you really do want what's best for each team member, it makes sense to hold everyone accountable. The team is only as strong as each individual team member, and if one person is not holding up his or her end of the bargain, it affects the entire group. It may seem easier to avoid hard conversations and discipline, but as Avery learned, it's not the responsible thing to do.

Avery's employees paid attention to what she did—and didn't do—when it came to conflicts within the team. Once she began to address problems and establish boundaries for team members, they came to respect her, because she was setting these expectations to help the team succeed. As Avery's story demonstrates, you can be thoughtful, kind, and caring and still hold people accountable. In fact, holding people accountable is often the thoughtful, kind, and caring thing to do!

As a leader, don't worry about pleasing everyone. People may like some of what you say or do some of the time and dislike it other times. If you're afraid people won't like you, it's hard to hold people accountable. And accountability is a leader's responsibility. Make the tough decisions when necessary, hold people accountable, and loosen the reins when you can.

Naturally, you don't want to err on the opposite side and be mean, insensitive, or callous, either. Be fair, interested, and supportive. If there are performance problems, deal with them. Resentment occurs when employees feel there is a double-standard and some employees are getting away with poor performance while others carry the load. It's crucial to be aware of who's doing what on your team and make sure all members are following through on their commitments. Slackers, spoilsports, and naysayers shouldn't have a place on your team. Work together with your employees to establish standards that are reasonable and that positively contribute to the performance of the team. Evaluate these standards and expectations on a regular basis to ensure they're relevant and viable.

Focus your attention on those employees who are doing their best and accomplishing great things. Look for and acknowledge what your team members are doing, each and every day. Your employees want you to notice them! So don't shy away from observing them in action. Do this so you can confidently point out the unique brilliance each employee contributes.

Whether you're a frontline supervisor, a manager, a director, or a CEO, remember that you're leading *people*. Be present and stay in the moment with team members. In this way, you'll be able to gauge what each person needs from you in a given situation, be it encouragement, resources, structure, information, or simply a bit of perspective and humor.

People can do amazing things under pressure and are willing to sacrifice to achieve lofty goals, but they can't sustain long periods of this. If you lose track of the people side of things and push people too much, too fast, and for too long, you will burn them out. At some point we all need to refresh, celebrate, and recuperate. Find that balance between setting standards and ensuring outcomes while motivating and supporting your employees. It's OK to ask for the moon; just give people a moon pie somewhere along the way.

You've been gifted a unique opportunity to lead others. Leadership is sometimes messy and confusing, and there's no way you can anticipate—and therefore avoid—all the unique pitfalls you'll encounter on your journey. But leadership is also rewarding and satisfying, because you're bound to open doors for others and positively impact their lives. Isn't that a rare privilege! If you lead with both your heart and your head, you'll find the possibilities for success are endless.

chapter 18

Afterword

IN THE EARLY SPRING OF 2020, as I completed the remaining chapters of this story, the novel coronavirus (COVID-19) unfolded, first across Asia, then Europe, then into the U.S. (and beyond), resulting in unparalleled deaths, economic destruction, and social upheaval. It was a leadership challenge none of us could ever imagine.

The pandemic threatened our lives and our livelihoods, forcing businesses to close and placing unwavering demands upon portions of the health care industry. It was a bleak and frightening time. Virtually no one was left untouched by the effects of the pandemic, which forced dramatic change upon most of the world. With required quarantines, then shelter-in-place restrictions, nonessential businesses shuttered and essential businesses that provided food, medicine, and basic services to the public were forced to work beyond the thresholds of their typical capacity. Government sent its workers home, to continue the work of governing from a distance as the rest of society tried to stay connected while living apart.

Despite the heartache of so many deaths from COVID-19, humans across the globe responded to the crisis with innovation and perseverance. It was a surreal experience that required a sudden adaptation to a new way of working and living. The imperative to "work from home" challenged us "average" people to innovate. And innovate we all did. Services once thought only possible in person were suddenly available via video format. We entertained each other, dated, attended AA meetings, and kept up with our meditation and yoga classes via Zoom and other online social media platforms.

Schools rapidly transitioned to an online format, and parents, for the first time in decades, found themselves responsible for the around-the-clock care, feeding, entertainment, and education of their children. Without the assistance of day care providers and teachers, parents worked from sunup to sundown, some of them interspersing the demands of their jobs with their parenting responsibilities. Years from now, parents will look back and reflect on the hardships and pressures they endured during this pandemic—the frustrations and long, weary days—but they'll also recall the depth of the parental bond they forged with their kids. Eating meals together became "a thing" again. We'll all watch to see the impact this crisis will have on what will, no doubt, be referred to as "Gen P" or the "pandemic generation."

Not all families fared well, because the pressures of forced isolation pushed some to the brink, resulting in increased levels of child and spousal abuse. In addition, job losses forced many, some for the first time in their lives, to file for unemployment insurance and seek out donations from soup kitchens and community food pantries. People lost incomes, homes, and careers. How will the historians describe these times? And what impact will this pandemic have on work, culture, politics, the environment, and the economy?

If you found yourself in a leadership position at any point during the 2020 pandemic, you experienced stressors and pressures like never before. Your employees needed you, but in vastly different ways. Some needed a level of compassion you probably weren't expecting, while others needed more of your time and attention. This wasn't the time to worry if you were "bugging" your employees by regularly checking in with them. Your sense that your employees were unusually needy was on target.

And despite the anxieties that most people were feeling, some of you were leading a team that was expected to continue to work as usual: accountants, payroll technicians, unemployment agents, police, firefighters, grocery stockers and clerks, and of course, those on the front lines of the pandemic: nurses, doctors, EMTs and the others who kept the COVID wards functioning for the ill. These frontline employees needed even different things from you. The pressures of the day muddied their brains and made concentration harder. They needed supervisors and managers who were understanding and compassionate, yet still motivated them to do good work. That's a tricky balance. You probably found that setting a regular schedule for a video call was a good idea. You probably kept your weekly team meetings via video call. You found ways to infuse a bit of fun into these calls. You did everything you could to support, encourage, and guide. Your middle name became "flexibility."

Hopefully, you also took time to care for yourself. Leadership can take a lot out of a person. The most effective leaders are other-oriented, and during normal times they're more apt to set their own needs aside. But in dangerous or tumultuous times, leaders must be sensitive to their own needs, as well as the needs of others. You need more sleep. Less booze. Less news and more comedy. You need a supportive colleague and a good friend to lean on. You need a routine that includes exercise and quiet time to reflect. You need yoga and meditation and good, healthy food.

If we learned anything through this pandemic, it's to reprioritize what truly matters. Work is important, but it cannot and should not be our full identities, because when or if we lose our work, we must still have a solid sense of self. Work, therefore, should be a way to use our strengths and give back in some way. It should provide us with a sense of accomplishment and satisfaction. It could help others, as we also help ourselves. Too many people lost their jobs from the shutdowns associated with the pandemic and felt "lost." Work should be an integral part of our lives, but not our entire lives.

We hopefully learned, from the shelter-in-place and self-quarantining requirements, to slow down a bit and live more simply. Dining out is a pleasure and a treat but probably is less of a regular event in many of our lives. Staying home, for a lot of us, became a painful experience—a boring experience—because we often live so much of our lives in different places: gyms, bars, restaurants, museums, art studios, hair salons, movie theatres, retail stores, and grocery stores. This time to ourselves or with our families gave us time to forge new hobbies and rediscover old ones. We had time on our hands and were meant to fill it.

The pandemic also forced many organizations and leaders to re-examine our relationships with work. Whether we liked it or not, we learned that "yes, we can do this successfully from home." Many who were longtime opponents of the work-from-home campaign were forced to trust that our employees were, indeed, working.

Things didn't get done as quickly or as perfectly as we would have liked, and in many cases, we had to accept that. And it turned out to be OK. High standards are important to strive for, but the pandemic made many of us relax our expectations.

We also had to rethink how we work and when. When all your team members are now free to work—on their own time and in their own way—and they still manage to produce a respectable product or service, you may need to admit that there are different ways to accomplish the same outcome. Your constant oversight? No longer necessary. Lesson learned.

As I worked to complete this manuscript, suddenly, in the midst of this dreadful disease threatening our lives and livelihoods, I thought to myself, *Well, all of this book is now moot.* And because I was stuck inside, I threw myself a nice little pity party. But then my thoughts turned to hope, partly because of the endless effort I put into this work, and partly because I know the material and the lessons in this story are useful and will remain useful for years to come. The strategies and approaches Jon and Avery learn and utilize are the foundation of effective leadership, regardless of whether you're leading an in-person team, a virtual one, or some combination of the two.

For example, as a leader, don't waste any opportunity to build trusting and respectful relationships with the people on your team. You have a unique opportunity to affect how people feel about themselves. Use your position to encourage those around you. Point out their brilliance and help them put their skills to use in ways they never thought possible. By doing so, you will help others become better versions of themselves.

Explore and tap into the diversity on your team, as it's one of your team's core strengths. Learn about the differences and similarities among team members. Embrace the weirdness that occurs when people are different. Cultivate that sensation and allow difference a voice on your team. You'll all grow to appreciate each other even more if you foster a genuine appreciation for difference.

Some leaders may balk at the importance of building relationships with their employees, but please don't be deceived. If you learn about your employees' passions and strengths, you can harness the energy that happens when people do what they love, regardless of the task.

No matter how quickly our workplaces change, one constant remains: the importance of open and timely communication. There are so many options for communication these days! No matter what form of communication you choose—tweets, texts, emails, or phone calls—none are as effective as face-to-face communication. There's something about eye contact and physical presence that sweetens the communication process. I recommend that you use a variety of communication media with your team. However, if you take only one piece of advice from this story, please let it be to go out of your way to meet consistently and regularly with each of your employees. As Avery discovered, this strategy creates a natural opportunity to talk more, share more, and exchange ideas together, which then results in healthier relationships.

Coaching will become your go-to strategy once you begin to develop trusting relationships with your employees. As Jon learned, the most effective leaders are not there to "show up" their employees, but instead to "shore up" their employees. Find ways to observe your employees "at work and in action" so you can acknowledge their contributions. Be generous with your praise and strategic with helpful feedback to leave the legacy of confidence and competence with your employees.

In times of crisis, leadership is even more crucial. Leaders are the voice of reason, painting a portrait of what can and will come, and pointing out the light in the distance that the rest of us can't yet see. One of the most important lessons from this book is to always be anticipating and forward-looking. Avery made the bold decision to move her team into a virtual environment, even though it wasn't needed at the time. Anticipating future needs and preparing your team with skills that will serve them down the road is an important leadership skill. Leaders never rest on their laurels or consider their work complete but rather keep their teams focused on the future.

Finally, don't sweat the small stuff. No one is perfect, as Jon and Avery both discovered. Mistakes are inevitable, and when they happen, talk it out, learn from it, and move on. Show grace and forgiveness toward others when they err and be open about your own failings. At the end of the workweek, or at the end of the pandemic, what really matters is how we feel about one another. So be mindful that even though you're a leader, you share the sidewalk with the rest of your team. You don't always have to be in front of them to be effective. Let someone else lead the way.

With all this said, there is one final truth that won't change as a result of the 2020 pandemic, or any other future crisis: leadership matters.

Your leadership will make a difference in the lives of your employees, colleagues, and community when you build strong relationships, support others, and help them become the best they can be. Our communities need this kind of powerful leadership now, more than ever.

I pray that you and your family, friends, colleagues, and staff maintain a positive attitude and a healthy mindset. Keep yourself well, and help others do the same, so we can all live with satisfying relationships, fulfilling work, and a future that inspires us all to continue the journey.

acknowledgments

I'VE NEVER WORKED ON SUCH A COMPLEX and exciting endeavor, so I didn't realize how many people would support, encourage, guide, and cajole me through the process of writing a book.

I chose to situate this story within a water utility, featuring characters from different fields: one from the distribution side of the industry and another in accounting. However, to be truthful, I have never replaced a shorn pipe (or used a clamp to fix a leaky one), and I'm no accountant (most things in my life rarely add up). I'm grateful that James Roche, Patricia Brubaker, Cindy Goodburn, and Leah Ash shared their expertise and made sure the industry-specific details in this story ring true. Through my association with longtime classroom collaborator Richard Gerstberger, I came to understand the challenges and nuances of the industry. I'm grateful to the many participants in my workshops who shared their experiences, struggles, and ideas with me. They gave me a broader understanding of the pitfalls and possibilities associated with leadership.

My colleagues in finance and accounting, especially Catrina Asher, Don Warn, and Jennifer Pike, also helped ensure that details in this book are accurate and realistic. I consider my friend and mentor, Sue Eaton, responsible for my understanding of all things related to Human Resources. Over the years, she's supported and encouraged me in my professional endeavors and has been an influential role model. And I can't forget to thank Marty Linsky, professor at the Harvard University Kennedy School of Government, for his insights and thoughtful suggestions which greatly improved this work.

Many years ago, I stood in front of a classroom with my colleague, Rob Moody, and delivered my first leadership workshop. Since then, I've had the privilege to work with and learn from many other experts in the field of leadership development. I'm grateful to all of you who so willingly shared your wisdom and partnered with me.

My best friend, Barbara Snakenberg, gave me a safe and quiet room of my own so I could complete this project. I'm quite certain there were times she thought I was napping or goofing off in the back room instead of doing any actual writing. She never complained and left me alone to write, and for that I'm very thankful. Tina Scardina read partial or full drafts and encouraged me to keep writing. In case you're wondering, words of support are really important to those of us pounding away at the keyboard.

The universe seems to bring the people, places, and circumstances together when creativity needs to flourish. That was the case for me when Polly Letofsky, of My Word Publishing, introduced me to my editor, Bobby Haas. It takes a certain amount of creative genius, coupled with commitment to the craft, to edit the work of a new writer and have it turn out as well as this book has. I'm continually amazed by his knowledge of writing and his eye as an editor.

That this story has made it onto an actual—or virtual—bookshelf near you is a credit to his editorial artistry. His encouragement has meant the world to me.

about the author

KAREN MAIN IS PASSIONATE about ridding organizations of lousy leadership. Her educational programs and presentations offer clarity and practical advice to professionals as they cope with the pressures and demands of today's workplace.

Karen earned her academic credentials in sociology from the University of Denver and has pursued numerous professional certifications that assist her when advising clients across the country. Her company, Innovations in Training, offers a full suite of leadership and team development programs and webinars. Known for her high-impact, engaging, and relevant curriculum, Karen blends storytelling and humor with activities that move participants slightly outside their comfort zones, where deep learning occurs. She's received recognition from the Ash Center at Harvard's John F. Kennedy School of Government, the Mountain States Employers Council, and the Association for Talent Development.

To consult with Karen or book her for your next event, visit her website: karenmain.com. Connect with her on LinkedIn (theleadershipexpert) or follow her on Twitter (@karemain) or Instagram (karenlmain).

notes

1   Geil Browning, *Emergenetics: Tap Into the New Science of Success (New York: Harper Collins, 2005)*. Emergenetics is a psychometric instrument designed by Geil Browning and Wendell Williams. For more information on the instrument, http://www.emergenetics.com.

2   Amy Gallo, "Why Aren't You Delegating?" *Harvard Business Review*, July 26, 2012, https://hbr.org/2012/07/why-arent-you-delegating .

3   Kenneth Blanchard, William Oncken, Jr. and Hal Burrows, *The One Minute Manager Meets the Monkey* (New York: HarperCollins, 1989), 97-99.

4   Patrick Lencioni, *The Five Dysfunctions of a Team: A Leadership Fable,* (San Francisco: Jossey-Bass, 2002).

5   Kenneth W. Thomas and Ralph H. Kilmann, *Thomas–Kilmann Conflict Mode Instrument* (Tuxedo, New York: Xicom, 1974), https://www.themyersbriggs.com/en-US/Products-and-Services/TKI .

6   Patterson, Kerry and Joseph Grenny, *Crucial Conversations Tools for Talking When Stakes Are High*, (NY: McGraw-Hill, 2012).

7   Marcus Buckingham and Curt Coffman, *First, Break All the Rules* (New York: Simon & Schuster, 1999).

8   Buckingham and Coffman, *First, Break All the Rules*, 223.

9   In late 1999 Ken Blanchard (Executive Education Publishers) published "Catch People Doing Something Right," which highlights this principle. No doubt there are numerous earlier references to this principle and since the publication of Blanchard's book, numerous other references to this general principle can be found in the contemporary literature on management and leadership.

10 Buckingham and Coffman, *First, Break All the Rules*, p. 154.

11 Buckingham and Coffman, *First, Break All the Rules*, p. 57.

12 Buckingham and Coffman, *First, Break All the Rules*, 58-59.